Sara Dunn is a writer and editor. She studied English Literature at Cambridge and has worked for a variety of environmental organisations including the International Institute for Environment and Development. Her articles have appeared in both national newspapers and environmental journals and she has acted as editorial consultant on a range of projects on green issues. She lives in London.

Alan Scholefield is a Canadian living in London. He studied English Literature at Oxford after which he worked in theatre on the fringe as an actor, director and teacher. He is now a freelance editor, and also helps run a well known specialist record shop in London.

D0542425

BENEATH THE WIDE WIDE HEAVEN

Poetry of the Environment
From antiquity to the present

Edited by Sara Dunn
with Alan Scholefield

To Thomas S. J. Dunn
and to Nancy Kendall

Acknowledgements

Many people have made invaluable contributions to the various stages of this book. I would like to thank: Melanie Silgardo and Becky Swift at Virago for the initial proposal and encouragement; Lavinia Greenlaw for sharing the work in early stages; Susan Bassnett, Margaret Busby, Jean Carlomusto, Arthur Clegg, Sue Clifford, Helen Dunmore, Angela King, Christian McEwan, Richard McKane, Sue O'Sullivan, Alison Read, Cherry Smyth, Susan Swift and Brenda Walker for suggestions for people and poems; Alison Read for much work on permissions; Sally Ramsden for enthusiastically undertaking the biographies; the staff at the South Bank's Poetry Library, in particular Dolores Conway, for dealing so gracefully with my endless queries; and my agent John Parker for much help and advice. In particular I would like to thank Mitch Cleary and Nel Druce for patience, practical help and much support. Finally, thanks to Alan Scholefield for being a joy to work with.

S. D.

My thanks to Sara, for the invitation, and for the happiness of working together; to the Honest Jon's massive for giving me the time to do this, and keeping me in the mix; and to Leah and Ben for everything.

A. S.

Published by VIRAGO PRESS Limited 1991
20–23 Mandela Street, Camden Town, London NW1 0HQ

This collection copyright © Sara Dunn 1991

A CIP catalogue record for this title
is available from the British Library

Printed in Great Britain by
The Guernsey Press Co. Ltd, Guernsey, Channel Islands

Acknowledgements for all copyright material are given
on pages 235–242, which constitute an extension of this
copyright page.

Now, my friends emerge
Beneath the wide wide Heaven – and view again
The many-steepled tract magnificent
Of hilly fields and meadows and the sea . . .

This Lime-Tree Bower My Prison
Samuel Taylor Coleridge

Contents

Introduction

Celebration
'So I shake with joy'

Kathleen Raine	'THE VERY LEAVES OF THE ACACIA-TREE ARE	
	LONDON'	3
Nazim Hikmet	FABLE OF FABLES	3
Langston Hughes	DREAM VARIATION	5
Uvavnuk	MOVED	6
Walt Whitman	*FROM* SONG OF MYSELF	6
Hugh MacDiarmid	*FROM* SCOTTISH SCENE	7
Boris Pasternak	STEPPE	8
Henry Thoreau	LOW-ANCHORED CLOUD	10
Geoffrey Chaucer	*FROM* THE PARLIAMENT OF FOWLS	10
'Abd Allah ibn al-Simak	THE GARDEN	11
Alden Nowlan	SACRAMENT	12
Margaret Walker	MY MISSISSIPPI SPRING	13
Denise Levertov	SPRING IN THE LOWLANDS	13
Olga Broumas	FOR ROBBIE MOORE	14
Praxilla	'MOST BEAUTIFUL OF THINGS'	14
Gerard Manley Hopkins	'REPEAT THAT, REPEAT'	15
John Clare	PLEASANT SOUNDS	15
William Cowper	*FROM* THE TASK, BOOK I	16
Percy Bysshe Shelley	*FROM* EPIPSYCHIDION	17
Sappho	'LEAVE KRETE AND COME TO THIS HOLY TEMPLE'	18
Michael Drayton	*FROM* POLY-OLBION, THE FIRST SONG	19
Wendy Rose	MOUNT SAINT HELENS/LOOWIT:	
	AN INDIAN WOMAN'S SONG	20
Friedrich Hölderlin	'YOU FIRMLY BUILT ALPS'	21
William Wordsworth	COMPOSED UPON WESTMINSTER BRIDGE	23
Anne Wilson	*FROM* TEISA: A DESCRIPTIVE POEM OF THE RIVER	
	TEES, ITS TOWNS AND ANTIQUITIES	23
Abraham Cowley	A PARAPHRASE UPON THE TENTH EPISTLE OF	
	THE FIRST BOOK OF HORACE	25
Gerard Manley Hopkins	INVERSNAID	26

James Thomson   FROM THE SEASONS, WINTER   26
Basho   'YEAR'S END'   27
W. H. Davies   A BRIGHT DAY   28

Loss
'Lament for all that is purple like dusk'

Gerard Manley Hopkins BINSEY POPLARS   31
Cassiano Ricardo   THE SONG OF THE WILD DOVE   32
Dorothy Parker   TEMPS PERDU   32
Ahmad 'Abd al
  Mu'ti Hijází   CAPTION TO A LANDSCAPE   33
Janice Gould   DISPOSSESSED   34
Jorge Carrera Andrade BIOGRAPHY FOR THE USE OF THE BIRDS   35
Margaret Walker   OCTOBER JOURNEY   36
Anon [Medieval Latin] FROM THE CAMBRIDGE SONGS   39
Wendy Rose   LONG DIVISION: A TRIBAL HISTORY   40
Claude McKay   THE TROPICS IN NEW YORK   41
John Clare   ENCLOSURE   41
Virgil   PASTORAL I   43
Michael Drayton   FROM PASTORALLS, THE FOURTH EGLOGUE   45
Adrienne Rich   STUDY OF HISTORY   46
Douris   EPHESOS   47
Elizabeth Weston   CONCERNING THE FLOODING OF PRAGUE AFTER
                         CONSTANT RAINS   48
George Awoonor-Williams THE SEA EATS THE LAND AT HOME   49
John Ceiriog Hughes   THE MOUNTAIN STREAM   50
Anon [Eskimo]   'FAR INLAND'   50
W. S. Graham   LOCH THOM   51

Anger
'A perpetual/sour October'

Helen Dunmore   PLOUGHING THE ROUGHLANDS   55
Wendell Berry   'I GO FROM THE WOODS'   56
Stevie Smith   ALONE IN THE WOODS   57
Tom Murray   CUTTING A TRACK TO CARDWELL   57
Charlotte Mew   THE TREES ARE DOWN   58
Elizabeth Carter   TO A GENTLEMAN, ON HIS INTENDING TO CUT
                         DOWN A GROVE TO ENLARGE HIS PROSPECT   59

Norman Nicholson	THE ELM DECLINE	61
Alexander Pope	FROM AN ESSAY ON MAN	63
Andrew Marvell	THE MOWER AGAINST GARDENS	63
Stevie Smith	'I LOVE THE ENGLISH COUNTRY SCENE'	64
H. D.	SHELTERED GARDEN	65
Patrick Magill	FROM PADDING IT	67
Charles Cotton	FROM THE WONDERS OF THE PEAKE	67
Maria Logan	VERSES ON HEARING THAT AN AIRY AND PLEASANT SITUATION, NEAR A POPULOUS AND COMMERCIAL TOWN, WAS SURROUNDED WITH NEW BUILDINGS	68
Ernesto Cardenal	NEW ECOLOGY	68
Anna Seward	FROM COLEBROOK DALE	71
Marion Bernstein	A SONG OF GLASGOW TOWN	73
Juvenal	FROM SATIRE III	74
Margaret Walker	SORROW HOME	75
Thadious M. Davis	'HONEYSUCKLE WAS THE SADDEST ODOR OF ALL, I THINK'	76
R. S. Thomas	AUTUMN ON THE LAND	78
Sylvia Plath	GREEN ROCK, WINTHROP BAY	78
Sheenagh Pugh	AFTER I CAME BACK FROM ICELAND	79
Terri Meyette	CELEBRATION 1982	80
Martyn Crucefix	MIKHAEL AT VIKSJÖN	81

Consolation
'Moments of an azure hue'

John Clare	COME HITHER	85
Claude McKay	AFTER THE WINTER	86
W. B. Yeats	THE LAKE ISLE OF INNISFREE	87
Charlotte Brontë	SPEAK OF THE NORTH	88
Frances Bellerby	PLASH MILL, UNDER THE MOOR	88
Rainer Maria Rilke	EARLY SPRING	89
Anna Akhmatova	TASHKENT BREAKS INTO BLOSSOM	90
Anna Akhmatova	'EVERYTHING IS PLUNDERED . . .'	91
Mieczyslaw Jastrun	BEYOND TIME	91
Anon [Eskimo]	DELIGHT IN NATURE	92
John Keats	ON THE GRASSHOPPER AND CRICKET	93
Byron	FROM CHILDE HAROLD'S PILGRIMAGE	93
Kathleen Raine	HEIRLOOM	95
Paula Gunn Allen	KOPIS'TAYA	96

Joyce Isabel Lee	GRANITE CALL	98
Charles Tomlinson	THE MARL PITS	99
Yüan Chieh	STONE FISH LAKE	99
William Barnes	TREES BE COMPANY	100
William Drummond	'THRISE HAPPIE HEE, WHO BY SOME SHADIE GROVE'	102
John Milton	*FROM* PARADISE LOST, BOOK IV	102
Mary Leapor	A SUMMER'S WISH	103
Lenrie Peters	AUTUMN BURNS ME	104
Henry Thoreau	WITHIN THE CIRCUIT OF THIS PLODDING LIFE	105
Ivor Gurney	THE SOAKING	106
Edward Thomas	DIGGING	107
Po Chü-I	PLANTING BAMBOOS	108
Anyte	'LOUNGE IN THE SHADE OF THE LUXURIANT LAUREL'S'	108

Contemplation

'How can you realise the wideness of the world?'

Theodore Roethke	THE ROSE	111
Pat Lowther	COAST RANGE	115
Po Chü-I	HAVING CLIMBED TO THE TOPMOST PEAK OF THE INCENSE-BURNER MOUNTAIN	117
Sylvia Plath	ABOVE THE OXBOW	118
Elizabeth Bishop	LESSON VI, LESSON X	120
Rosemary Dobson	DRY RIVER	121
Molly Holden	SO WHICH IS THE TRUTH?	122
Liz Lochhead	INNER	123
Pablo Neruda	OH EARTH, WAIT FOR ME	127
Emily Dickinson	'"NATURE" IS WHAT WE SEE'	128
Goethe	EPIRRHEMA	128
Rose Flint	CONNECTIONS	129
Anne Finch	A NOCTURNAL REVERIE	129
Elinor Wylie	WILD PEACHES	131
Gillian Allnut	SUNART	133
Ralph Waldo Emerson	HAMATREYA	134
J. Kitchener Davies	*FROM* THE SOUND OF THE WIND THAT IS BLOWING	136
Charles Tomlinson	AT STOKE	138
Czeslaw Milosz	ADVICE	138
Amy Clampitt	THE REEDBEDS OF THE HACKENSACK	139

Molly Holden	PIECES OF UNPROFITABLE LAND	140
Mary Ursula Bethell	PAUSE	141
Sheenagh Pugh	GEOGRAPHY 2	142
Alice Walker	ON SIGHT	142
Angelina Weld Grimké	THE BLACK FINGER	143
Adrienne Rich	RURAL REFLECTIONS	143
Hans Magnus Enzensberger	LACHESIS LAPPONICA	144
Sylvia Plath	TWO CAMPERS IN CLOUD COUNTRY	147
Wallace Stevens	THIS SOLITUDE OF CATARACTS	148

Observation
'Sensitive to the millionth of a flicker'

Hsü Ling	THE WATERS OF LUNG-T'OU	151
Norman MacCaig	SIGNS AND SIGNALS	151
Les A. Murray	THE GUM FOREST, *FROM* FOUR GAELIC POEMS	152
Emily Dickinson	'BLAZING IN GOLD'	153
John Pepper Clark	IBADAN	154
C. P. Cavafy	MORNING SEA	154
Eldred Revett	LAND-SCHAP BETWEEN TWO HILLS	154
dsh	CONCRETE POEM 240663	156
Elizabeth Bishop	THE BIGHT	157
Elizabeth Coatsworth	WHALE AT TWILIGHT	158
R. S. Thomas	NIGHT AND MORNING	158
Pablo Neruda	THE NIGHT IN ISLA NEGRA	159
Tomas Tranströmer	FROM MARCH '79	159
Alice Sadongei	WHAT FRANK, MARTHA AND I KNOW ABOUT THE DESERT	160
Anon [Yoruba]	RIDDLES	161
Anon [Mudbara]	'THE DAY BREAKS'	162
Rosario Morales	¡ROBLES, M'HIJA, ROBLES!	162
Robert Bly	DRIVING TOWARD THE LAC QUI PARLE RIVER	163
Gary Snyder	THE TRAIL IS NOT A TRAIL	164
Olga Broumas	ROADSIDE	165
Seamus Heaney	THE ROAD AT FROSSES	165
Emily Dickinson	'AS IMPERCEPTIBLY AS GRIEF'	166
Laury Wells	THE NOMADS	167
Edith Södergran	NOCTURNE	167
Anon [Ewe]	THE SKY	168

Disquiet
'Something warns me everywhere'

Ruth Fainlight	THE POWER SOURCE	171
Gillian Clarke	NEIGHBOURS	172
Helen Dunmore	PERMAFROST	173
Anna Akhmatova	'DISTANCE COLLAPSED IN RUBBLE'	175
Seamus Heaney	AUGURY	175
Alden Nowlan	ST JOHN RIVER	176
Michael Hamburger	A DREAM OF WATER	176
Liz Lochhead	WHAT THE POOL SAID, ON MIDSUMMER'S DAY	178
Stevie Smith	THE RIVER GOD	180
U. A. Fanthorpe	RISING DAMP	181
Ray A. Young Bear	THE REASON WHY I AM AFRAID EVEN THOUGH I AM A FISHERMAN	183
Raymond Carver	THE RIVER	184
Andrew Young	THE FEAR	185
Frances Horovitz	WINTER WOODS	185
Frances Horovitz	WALKING IN AUTUMN	186
Stevie Smith	OUT OF TIME	187
Emily Dickinson	'THERE'S A CERTAIN SLANT OF LIGHT'	188
Denise Levertov	OVERHEARD OVER S. E. ASIA	189
Antoni Malczewski	OPEN SPACES	189
W. S. Rendra	TWILIGHT VIEW	190
David Jones	*FROM* IN PARENTHESIS	191
Ruth Fainlight	THE FIELD	192
Mahmud Darwish	WE ARE ENTITLED TO LOVE AUTUMN	193
Antonio Machado	TODAY'S MEDITATION	194
Hugh MacDiarmid	ONE OF THESE DAYS	195
Lavinia Greenlaw	THE RECITAL OF LOST CITIES	195
Charlotte Mew	DOMUS CAEDET ARBOREM	196
James Thomson	*FROM* THE CITY OF DREADFUL NIGHT	197
Alfonsina Storni	MEN IN THE CITY	198
Margaret Atwood	A HOLIDAY	199
Issa	'NEVER FORGET'	200
Elaine Feinstein	BY THE CAM	200
George Crabbe	*FROM* THE POOR OF THE BOROUGH, LETTER XXII, PETER GRIMES	201
Thomas Hardy	NIGHT-TIME IN MID-FALL	202
John Milton	*FROM* PARADISE LOST, BOOK II	203
James Thomson	*FROM* THE SEASONS, SUMMER	205
Kwesi Brew	THE DRY SEASON	205

Robert Penn Warren   SUMMER STORM (CIRCA 1916), AND GOD'S
                             GRACE   206
King James Bible   JEREMIAH 4, 23–28   207
Nina Cassian   AND WHEN SUMMER COMES TO AN END . . .   208

Biographical Notes   211
Acknowledgements   235
Index of Poets   243
Index of First Lines   245

Introduction

From going to and fro on the earth
And from walking up and down on it . . .

Book of Job

One of the curiouser effects of the contemporary explosion in environmental concern is that it has caused the very term 'environment' to
become simultaneously both abstracted and contracted. In the industrial
world environmental topics seem to be collapsed in the popular imagina-
tion into a few issues, such as the destruction of the Brazilian rainforest and
the greenhouse effect. Somehow these topics are grabby, almost glamorous,
and what many regard as the fundamentals of environmentalism – the
affective relationships between each of us and our individual surroundings
– are lost in the vision of global apocalypse. Environment has almost come
to mean something 'somewhere else'.

In this collection we have tried to go back to the fundamentals. This is
not to deny the terribly urgency of large-scale problems, or the desirability
– indeed necessity – of a global approach to them; but our aim in this
anthology is to give space to a more localised view of our environment.
We have concentrated on focused views, rooted in the immediacy of
poets' external worlds. They reflect experience that is often quotidian, certainly centred around the individual. Ultimately, we believe, they are more
empowering as a result. In taking this approach we hope to re-emphasise
the concept of environment as constant and contiguous, not a 'bundle of
issues' but something all of us experience, in our daily 'toing and froing on
the earth', and have a right to some control over.

★   ★   ★

We've never, no, not for a single day,
pure space before us, such as that which flowers
endlessly open into.

Rainer Maria Rilke, 'The Eighth Elegy'

One of our personal aims in putting together this anthology is to find some comfort in a subject whch has become, at times, unbearably bleak. The doom-laden prognostications which, though hardly new, have achieved such currency in the late 1980s and 1990s, have a numbing effect and often seem counter-productive, inducing a sort of environmental compassion-fatigue. It seems that the 'facts' about environmental problems can now be regarded as 'common knowledge', and their effects on humans as inescapable, if not always predictable. If this is so, why is it that nothing really seems to change?

When it comes to solutions, much environmentalist literature – although passionate, informed and utterly convincing on environmental problems – subsides into rather insipid discussions about values, to the effect that if we only changed our hearts a little and loved the planet and each other all would be well. The crudeness of this approach lies in its inability to exam-ine how such values came to be adopted in the first place – *why* we feel as we do about our surroundings.

How we see our environment and 'what we do about it' is a function not of what is 'really out there' but how we perceive it. Ten years ago I had a relatively uncomplicated enjoyment of 'the countryside', both agri-cultural and uncultivated land. The same pieces of land can now depress me profoundly, as I see everywhere signs of environmental degradation – signs which were very possibly there before, but which I did not have the knowledge to interpret. The land has hardly changed, but my capacity to enjoy it has been transformed.

This is certainly not to suggest that ignorance is bliss, but is an illustra-tion – albeit an obvious one – of the essential interpenetration between landscape and human emotion. We never know the world as it is – Rilke's 'pure space before the flower' – only the world presented to us through our senses and mediated by experience and cultural values.

★   ★   ★

I wanted to be a nature poet
And write hauntingly of
Southern landscapes
Lush with brilliant birds . . .

I forgot 'Poplar trees bear a
Strange Fruit'
Deep roots
Strong limbs
Flexing
Spreading
North
Searing cultured descendants of
Fiery abolitionists . . .

Thadious M. Davis, 'Honeysuckle was the saddest odor of all, I think'

A central metaphor of ecological debate is that of 'spaceship earth'. The planet is seen as a closed and global ecosystem in which we are all passengers; all humans are 'in the same boat'. This global projection is often the clarion call to environmental action, but it can, albeit on occasions unwittingly, steer us into some rather dubious ideological territory. As Hans Magnus Enzensberger says:

> The ideological purpose of such hasty global projections is clear. The aim [of the spaceship earth metaphor] is to deny once and for all that little difference between first class and steerage, between the bridge and the engine room.
>
> *Dreamers of the Absolute*, p.271

The matrix of gender, race, class and the other definitions which constitute all our identities will profoundly affect how each of us sees the environment, and a genuinely productive approach to the politics of environment will pay close attention to these views and how they are arrived at. Looking at poetic landscapes, each so individual, described from varying cultural stances by both women and men, is one route towards some understanding of the differing 'psychologies' of environmentalism, and, we hope, a move away from some of the cruder assumptions behind our present sense of crisis.

★   ★   ★

> The charming landscape which I saw this morning is indubitably made up of some twenty or thirty farms. Miller owns this field, Locke that, and Manning the woodland beyond. But none of them owns the landscape. There is a property in the horizon which no man [sic] has but he whose eye can integrate all the parts, that is, the poet.

> Ralph Waldo Emerson, *Nature*, 1836

Poetry is an inclusive medium. This inclusivity – Emerson's 'integration of the parts' – together with distilled subjectivity, avoidance of the doctrinaire, and resistance of dichotomies (avoiding the simplistic distinction between what is natural and what is unnatural, what is rural and what is urban) make poetry an invaluable tool with which to explore the nature of human interaction with the external world.

Emerson saw it as the duty of the poet to reveal the beauty and value of new things, including science, technology and industry; and contemporary British poet Helen Dunmore catches the spirit of this resistance of division in an essay in her collection *The Raw Garden*:

> If the garden of Eden really exists it does so moment by moment, fragmented and tough, cropping up like a fan of buddleia high up in the gutter of a deserted warehouse, or in a heap of frozen cabbages becoming luminous in the reflected light of roadside snow.

> 'Code-breaking in the Garden of Eden', *The Raw Garden* p. 60

★   ★   ★

The Western environmental movement has a tendency to assert the existence of an era in the (often unspecified) past when humankind had a more benign attitude to nature, when there was a more 'even balance' between humans and the world around them. This is by no means a new phenomenon; in 1793 Maria Logan mourns the passing of a harmonious rural way of life:

> There was a time! that time the Muse bewails,
> When Sunny Hill enjoyed refreshing gales;
> When Flora sported in its fragrant bowers,

And strewed with liberal hand her sweetest flowers!

Maria Logan, 'Verses on hearing that an airy and pleasant situation . . . was
surrounded with new buildings', 1793

In 1593 in his 'Fourth Eglogue' Michael Drayton described the golden
age in times past when:

The tender grasse was then the softest bed:
The pleasant'st shades esteem'd the statelyest halls.

In his famously eloquent introductory passage to *The Country and the
City*, Raymond Williams finds himself on a historical 'escalator' forever
moving backwards through English history, past writer after writer asserting
the existence of an idyllic rural bygone age, always 'just over the last hill'.

It is hard to pin down what this looking backwards actually constitutes
in relation to the environment. In part it seems to be a simple nostalgia, an
ill-defined yearning for the past. Freud noted the phenomenon; in his
General Introduction to Psychoanalysis he takes up the nostalgic feeling we
often attach to the 'unspoiled' landscape as an illustration of our chronic
yearning to enjoy 'freedom from the grasp of the external world'. He
regards this as the epitome of phantasy-making:

The creation of the mental domain of phantasy has a counterpart in
the establishment of 'reservations' and 'nature-parks' in places where
the inroads of agriculture, traffic or industry threaten to change . . .
the earth into something unrecognizable. The 'reservation' is to
maintain the old condition of things which has been regretfully
sacrificed to necessity everywhere else . . .

Sigmund Freud, *A General Introduction to Psychoanalysis*, 1920
(Quoted in Leo Marx, *The Machine and the Garden*, 1964, p.8)

This is not a modern phenomenon, but it *does* rely on an urban sensi-
bility. Virgil's *Eclogues*, the fountainhead of all pastoral, are predicated precisely on the tension between the idyllic rural setting and the world of
chaos and urban politics beyond:

Beneath the shade which beechen boughs diffuse
You, Tityrus, entertain your sylvan muse.
Round the wide world in banishment we roam.
Forced from our pleasing fields and native home . . .

> Virgil, 'Pastoral I', trans. John Dryden

The ideal landscape is sketched in only to be framed in an alien and encroaching world; even here the rural myth is threatened by an incursion of history. At the end nothing is solved – the poem offers not the slightest hint of a way out for Meliboeus or those who inhabit the countryside. Virgil's unruffled, contemplative tone is used to imply that the episode belongs to a timeless recurrent pattern in human affairs – and the tone is sophisticated, urbane.

★   ★   ★

spill vision
After the horizons, stretching the narrowed eye
To full capacity.

> Sylvia Plath, 'Above the Oxbow'

Because we wanted to be wide-ranging in historical and cultural terms, our definition of 'the environment' has had to exclude some areas: we have not included poems primarily concerned with animals – a discrete topic and one well-anthologised. We have also limited material in terms of 'scale': we have chosen, for example, poems about gardens rather than those about dahlias; poems about city streets and townscapes rather than individual buildings or interiors. This is all poetry of the outdoor environment with some sense of horizon; the gaze is one with a degree of width – more landscape than still-life. Beyond that, we have tried to make the landscapes as diverse as possible with cities, countrysides, wildernesses and gardens, from the Downs of England to Australian gum forests, New York to Ibadan, the Incense Burner Mountain to the Adirondacks.

In a broadly thematic anthology with variety of response as its touchstone, a division according to 'emotional' states became the only logical one. We were well aware of the pitfalls in dividing this most ambiguous of forms of expression into tonal categories, but it soon became clear that ambiguities, far from being stifled by this process, were often brought out more forcibly by a defining context. The categories are not the last word on interpreting the poems, and the system is intended as an illumination – perhaps provocative – but not defining.

Celebration
'So I shake with joy'

The sky's height stirs me.
The strong wind blows through my mind.
It carries me with it,
so I shake with joy.

Uvavnuk, 'Moved'

Uvavnuk's chant tells how the immensity of the natural landscape moves her beyond self-control, and all the poems in this section express an unalloyed pleasure in the writers' surroundings. They range from the immediate, uncomplicated tactile joys of the natural environment explored by poems like Denise Levertov's 'Spring in the Lowlands' and Henry Thoreau's 'Low-Anchored Cloud' to the imagined pastoral paradise of Shelley's 'Epipsychidion'.

It is not always the natural environment which is celebrated; Wordsworth leaves his more accustomed mountains and woods to claim 'Earth has not anything to show more fair' than the city of London:

Never did sun more beautifully steep
In his first splendour, valley, rock, or hill.

'Composed on Westminster Bridge'

Hölderlin's fragmentary poem 'You Firmly Built Alps!' praises Stuttgart in the same tone as the Alps and the surrounding forests, sweeping up all features of his native Württemberg with a breathy and 'naive' intensity.

Michael Drayton also celebrates his native land – England – as he raises the island of Albion by classical allusion, to Olympian heights. The grand and consequently rather blurred description of 'Albion's glorious isle' contrasts both with Hölderlin's particular geography and with Hugh MacDiarmid's 'Scottish Scene', a smaller-scaled, detailed vision of his

native land, the land 'nae man can be dull in'. In many poems in this book
the landscape is a focus for particular human and group identities. For
example we can see patriotic sentiment divided into two categories, local
and imperial. Local patriotism, like MacDiarmid's, rests on the intimate
experience of place, and on a sense of its fragility – that which we love has
no guarantee to endure. Imperial patriotism feeds on collective egotism and
pride, and the sentiment tends not to attach itself to anything concretely
geographical. However, the collective thrust of these poems is to sweep
aside patriotism as a relevant category, and to proclaim other allegiances,
some regional and some not, some local and some universal.

Anne Wilson, writing in 1778, celebrates the 'improvement' of nature,
as previously unusable wetlands are reclaimed by human ingenuity:

> The rotten ground, which trembled as we trod,
> Is now released from the exuberant load . . .
> This plan would each landholder but pursue
> England a paradise we then might view.

'Teisa'

Horace's 'Letter to Aristius Fuscus', an early and eloquent celebration of
country life as opposed to town life (here paraphrased by Abraham
Cowley), decries the artificial control of water in the town:

> Does art through pipes a purer water bring,
> Than that which nature strains into a spring?

Horace's ideal landscape is a typical evocation of the pastoral ideal of tem-
perateness. Unlike Gerard Manley Hopkins' 'weeds and wilderness' it is
certainly not land untouched by humans, but a tended agricultural area.
This was the land most often celebrated by earlier writers. The ideal environment resisted all extremes, being neither hot nor cold, urban nor wild,
but a balance of all:

> Th'air of that place so attempre was
> That nevere was ther greveance of hot ne cold.

Geoffrey Chaucer, 'The Parliament of Fowls'

Abd Allah ibn al–Simak's garden reminds him of the beauty of religious faith, and much overtly celebratory environmental poetry is religious, as natural bounty represents the proof of divine providence of one kind or another. In spite of this the Judaeo-Christian inheritance (for example) with regard to nature is an ambivalent one; God's munificence as evidenced in nature is praised, but at the same time regarded as under human dominion:

> And God said, Behold I have given you every herb-
> yielding seed which is upon the face of the earth, and
> every tree, in which is the fruit of a tree yielding
> seed; to you it shall be for meat.

> *Genesis*, I, 29

Wendy Rose's 'Mount Saint Helen's/Loowit' turns the notion of dominion on its head, as the mountain is shown to be holding the planet – and all of us – in place, and the natural environment, possessed of superior wisdom, merely 'nods and waits'.

Loss
'Lament for all that is purple like dusk'

Hopkins' famous poem 'Binsey Poplars' laments both the felling of trees and the ignorance and clumsiness of human management of nature:

> even where we mean
> To mend her we end her
> When we hew or delve . . .

But, it is not the loss of natural landscapes alone that has engaged poets; human loss due to inimicable nature is just as much a topic as natural loss due to inimicable humans. Douris ('Ephesos'), Elizabeth Weston ('Concerning the Flooding of Prague after Constant Rains') and George Awoonor-Williams ('The Sea Eats the Land at Home') all lament the loss of human life in the face of uncontrollable nature, as water bursts out of its 'natural' boundaries and washes away feeble human habitations and lives.

The loss of a natural landscape is often inextricably fused with the passing of a way of life (as in John Clare's 'Enclosure'), or of a golden age (as in Michael Drayton's 'Fourth Eglogue'). Cassiano Ricardo's 'The Song of the Wild Dove' mourns all that is 'tall like palm trees', 'long like rivers' and 'purple like dusk' – and these things gesture towards some more abstract, unnameable human loss. In 'Temps Perdu' Dorothy Parker evokes this unnameable grief, of which she is consistently reminded by seemingly 'neutral' landscapes:

> The look of a laurel tree birthed for May
> Or a sycamore bared for a new November
> Is as old and as sad as my furtherest day –
> What is it, what is it, I almost remember?

Wendy Rose names the source of her grief precisely – the disappearance of her people, whose very bodies create the landscapes which others exclaim over:

> It's our blood that gives you
> those southwestern skies

> 'Long Division: A Tribal History'

Ahmad 'Abd al-Mu'ti Hijází sees the continuity of the landscape as a a sad reminder of his own changes – his loss of innocence and wonder:

> The picture is still clear
> But the child who drew it
> Has been crushed by the passages of days.

> 'Caption to a Landscape'

Anger
'A perpetual/sour October'

The anger in these poems has its main source in human impact on nature, but, as in the previous section, emotion is also directed at nature's intransigence towards people – as well as at 'bland philosophies' concerning the natural world – at nature-poets themselves, and at social inequalities which can taint or wholly obliterate enjoyment of the landscape.

Modern agricultural practice, creating its 'pale monoculture' (in Helen Dunmore's 'Ploughing the Roughlands') is one target, and tree clearing once again an emotive topic. Tom Murray sees the clearing of a track by white Australian settlers as an act as antipathetical and strange to him as their harsh-sounding language:

Cut to ground level
Trees in a wide swath
Cut to ground level
With steel axes
Cut so quickly
By a mob of men, chattering in English
Their voices echoing
English . . .

'Cutting a Track to Cardwell'

Anger over the cutting of trees has a long precedent; modern historical geographers have shown that the wild woods had gone from most of England, for example, even before the arrival of the Romans, and that by the end of the Anglo-Saxon period the bulk of forest clearance had been completed. It is hardly surprising that trees became increasingly cherished. In England, from the fifteenth century on they were valued not just for their practical uses, nor even their beauty, but because of their human meaning – what they symbolised to the community in terms of continuity and association.

Gardens occur as a very ambivalent symbol here; they can appear to be a recognition of the essential harmony of the natural order – as in Chaucer's garden in the 'Parliament of Fowls' – or a denial of it. The seventeenth-century English poet Andrew Marvell was particularly concerned with this ambiguity; in his 'mower poems' the cultivated garden is not an indication – as it is, for example in Milton – of an ordered universe, but is a vain, urban phenomenon, the product of 'luxuriant man'. 'The Mower Against Gardens' takes what feels like a very modern view of the impossibility of harmony between people and their environment:

And in the cherry he does nature vex
  To procreate without a sex
'Tis all enforced, the fountain and the grot,
  While the sweet fields do lie forgot.

'The Mower Against Gardens'

Patrick Magill sounds a loud counterblast to romantic notions of nature, attacking the privileged hypocrisy of 'nature poets' who praise the great outdoors but don't actually have to live with it. Of course some nature poets felt the 'uneducated' didn't really deserve to experience nature's beauty; the impetus, for example, behind Wordsworth's impassioned plea against the incursion of the Kendal and Windermere railway into the heart of the English Lakes was the fact that it threatened to flood the Lake District with 'the whole of Lancashire and no small part of Yorkshire'. The urban lower classes, Wordsworth felt, could derive no good from immediate access to the Lakes – they needed a preparatory course, starting with Sunday excursions in the nearby fields (see Wordsworth's *Guide to the Lakes*).

It is interesting to see what a complete reversal of feeling occurred between the Wordsworthian extreme reverence for mountainous scenery and Charles Cotton's *The Wonders of the Peake*:

A Country so deform'd, the Traveller
Would swear those parts Natures *pudenda* were.

Cotton was by no means untypical in seeing wildness as distasteful, as he takes the cult of earth as mother to its ultimate misogynist conclusions. Before 1700 most educated people found hilly country distasteful, infinitely preferring the tamed and fertile landscape – the farm or garden – over which people had asserted their control.

Cities, of course, have encountered the ire of many writers, and not just since the Industrial Revolution. Juvenal's famous satire on urban Rome ('Satire III') could be a modern rant against urban living, with its sub-standard housing, fire hazards and noise pollution – not to mention dangerous sanitation arrangements. In fact traffic congestion, pollution and bad housing conditions had been problems throughout the Roman empire, even before Juvenal's time. One of Julius Caesar's first acts on seizing power was to try to decrease the appalling congestion by banning wheeled traffic from the centre of Rome during the day, with the resulting devastating effect on the inhabitants' sleep.

Consolation
'Moments of an azure hue'

Nature has long been seen as the source of consolation in the face of the 'clamorous' (human) world. For Anna Akhmatova, 'misery gnaws to the bone', and she asks herself almost incredulously, 'Why then do we not despair?' Because:

> By day, from the surrounding woods,
> cherries blow summer into town . . .
>
> 'Everything is Plundered'

Consolation often comes in the form of an ideal environment fondly remembered or fervently imagined: McKay's 'quiet hill', Yeats' 'bee-loud glade' or Yüan Chieh's 'stone fish lake'. (For Milton's Satan in *Paradise Lost* the perfection of the Garden of Eden is sufficient to lift much of the suffering angel's unimaginable weight of sadness, but even nature cannot drive away Satan's worst sin – despair.)

Consolation can also be found in a comforting aspect of a landscape which had seemed comfortless. In 'Speak of the North' Charlotte Brontë's 'lonely moor / Silent and dark and trackless swells', a seemingly lifeless landscape, until suddenly a stag appears, to drink at a stream, and far away:

> . . . one star, large and soft and lone,
> Silently lights the unclouded skies.

In a similar terrain, the abandoned mill in Frances Bellerby's 'Plash Mill, Under the Moor' seems deserted, barren and sodden in the autumn wind until:

> next March, perhaps, sunlight the colour of frost
> Wavers through branches to honeycomb some flaking wall.

Henry Thoreau and Edward Thomas both derive comfort from their work on the land. Thoreau has momentary visions 'of an azure hue':

> Some unrecorded beam slanted across
> The unpaid pastures where the Johnswort grew.

> 'Within the Circuit of this Plodding Life'

While in 'Digging' Thomas feels it enough 'to smell, to crumble the dark earth'.

Paula Gunn Allen's 'Kopis'taya' laments the urban environment, where the 'heavy air' blocks the breath, but feels in the soft fall of a twilight rain intimations of other ways of living. The 'significant drops' carry with them the 'spirit voices', which 'weave dreams upon our shadowed skulls'. But they are not necessarily dreams of escape, for just as the stones of the earth once welcomed ancestral feet, so the spirit voices' feet now touch the cement of the city, 'the asphalt delighting'. The voices are there to be heard, here in the city, if only 'we could listen'.

Contemplation
'How can you realise the wideness of the world?'

'There are those to whom place is unimportant' says Theodore Roethke in 'The Rose'; the poets here are certainly not among them, as they all attempt to understand the importance of place and their relation to it. There is a constant movement between a sense of apartness and a sense of connectedness in all these poems; for Sylvia Plath in 'Above the Oxbow', climbing the Monadnock means reinforcing a separateness which brings with it a sense of perspective and order:

> all that unique
> Stipple of shifting wave-tips is ironed out, lost
> In the simplified orderings of sky –
> Lorded perspectives.

Up in the mountains humans can move 'coolly'.

In 'A Nocturnal Reverie' Anne Finch effects a withdrawal from worldly cares:

Till the free soul to a compos'dness charmed,
Finding the elements of rage disarmed,
O'er all below a solemn quiet grown,
Joys in th' inferior world and thinks it like her own

Her lines are very much in the tradition of seventeenth- and eighteenth-century rural retreat poems. Far from being straightforward paeans to rural living, these poems are often in fact consolatory pieces. Many of the best known rural idylls of the period were compensatory myths composed by or for unsuccessful politicians or disappointed careerists. The self-imposed political exile of Lord Fairfax at Nun Appleton inspired Andrew Marvell, and Anne Finch, having retired to the countryside because she was unable to reconcile herself to the English revolution of 1688, then composed poems celebrating the virtue of contented rural 'retirement'.

Hans Magnus Enzensberger is perhaps slightly less disingenuous in 'lachesis lapponica', as he finds himself unable to entertain thoughts of escape even for a moment, as the 'bird in his head' refuses to allow the existence of a landscape which blanks the mind:

here where i stand, that whiteness in the wind
      is the moor sedge
look how it flickers, the silent empty wilderness here
      is the earth.

(¡*viva!* cries the dusky bird: ¡*viva fidel castro!*)

The idea of wilderness as an essence devoid of social implications and politics is seen as always alluring and always impossible; getting away from it is not merely a luxury, it is an illusion.

Some poets highlight a sense of cooperation between people and their environments. J. Kitchener Davies reads a history of his people in the landscape they have husbanded and named:

My grandfather, said my father, had planted the Middle
      Fields – Cae Cwteri, Cae Polion, Cae Troi –
but generations we knew nothing at all about,
except for the mark of their handiwork on Cae Lloi and Cae Moch,
had planted the tall strong stout-trunked trees round the house,
and set sweet-plums here and there in the hedges.

In 'Geography 2' Sheenagh Pugh approaches the notion of husbandry 'from the other end', seeing the landscape deliberately forming itself in expectation of future use:

> A coast curved itself into a haven
> for shipping; a hill kept watch
> on the landscape till the fort was built.

Underlying this notion of 'landish' benevolence is a slightly uneasy disparity of scale: huge land masses 'crashed together' to make 'a border waiting for customs posts' – but we feel they could just as easily crash apart and the rather flimsy signs of human impact disappear once more.

Czeslaw Milosz, by contrast, has no notion of the kindness of the natural world, and rebukes anyone who looks back nostalgically to a time when nature was supposedly unspoiled and benign. According to him – apart from a possible moment 'when Adam woke', the beasts were friendly and their fangs merely 'figurative' – 'what we know of Nature':

> Does not speak in its favour. Ours is no worse.
> So I beg you, no more of those lamentations.

'Advice'

Many of the poets here resist bland distinctions between good land and bad land, ugly and beautiful, profitable and useless. Amy Clampitt's 'Reedbeds of the Hackensack' denies the urge to lament the ugliness of landfill:

> those Edens-in-the-work of the irrevocably ugly,
> where any mourning would of course be fraudulent

and in 'Pieces of Unprofitable Land' Molly Holden celebrates the 'memories of former wilds' evoked by the rough ground at the edge of fields, seeing in their unplanned, unharvested growth 'proof of reclamation'.

The capacity of land to 'go on without us' can of course be chastening as well as comforting. Emerson's earth

> laughs in flowers, to see her boastful boys
> Earth-proud, proud of the earth which is not theirs
> Who steer the plough, but cannot steer their feet
> Clear of the grave.

'Hamatreya'

Observation
'Sensitive to the millionth of a flicker'

To stop and actually to look at what is around is not as easy as it may appear. Just as Hans Magnus Enzensberger cannot make himself blank-brained in 'lachesis lapponica', so C.P. Cavafy admits he cannot take in what is around him for more than an initial moment:

> Let me stand here. And let me pretend I see all this
> (I actually did see it for a minute when I first stopped).

'Morning Sea'

In the course of observation poets are attempting to impose order; they are fighting not just with their own 'daydreams' – like Cavafy – but also with the randomness of what is around them. In eighteenth-century land-scape poetry, such as Eldred Revett's 'Land-schap between Two Hills', this poetic ordering was at its most overt.

> Some way the field thence swells at ease
> And lifts our sight up by degrees
> To where the steep side dissie lies
> Supinely fast in precipice
> Till with the bank oppos'd it lie,
> In a proportion'd Harmonise . . .

The history of the term 'landscape' itself encapsulates the complex process of ordering which occurs between the observer and the environment described; in the late-sixteenth century 'landskip' was a technical term used by painters to describe a rendering of an outdoor view. The term began to be applied to real places. The first example of its use to describe 'real' terrain given in the *OED* is by John Milton in *L'Allegro* in 1632. In the

seventeenth century the relationship between artistic perception and reality
became unbelievably dense; painters began to paint real views because they
looked like fine landscape paintings. By the eighteenth century an educated
person in Europe would have found it hard not only to describe land but
even to *think* of it except as mediated through highly formal visual rules.
The landscape demanded to be thought of as itself composed into the patterns which previously landscape painters had thought of as themselves
imposing on it.

The twentieth-century Scottish poet Norman MacCaig sees the natural
environment as manifesting not so much order, as meaning:

> . . . they unhurriedly wind
> Round the Loch of the Green Corrie
> And the Loch of the Wolf's Pass
> That are hung there in my mind
>
> And drenched with meaning . . .

'Signs and Signals'

The tools all poets must use to impose order or manifest meaning –
words – will perhaps always prove inadequate in the face of what is 'out
there':

> The wild does not have words.
> The unwritten pages spread themselves out in all
>   directions!
> I come across the marks of roe-deer's hooves in the
>   snow.
> Language but no words.

Tomas Tranströmer, 'From March '79'

Disquiet
'Something warns me everywhere'

This sense of hidden meaning, of a language without words, is at the heart
of the unease many poets describe when confronted with the natural landscape. Some natural environments seem to have changed their meaning by

losing their connection with nature – the 'power source has shifted' says Ruth Fainlight, who notices:

> the strain of trying
> to be a nature-poet
> these unbucolic days.

'The Power Source'

But it is by no means always 'disturbed' nature that unnerves us. Raymond Carver, for example, fears the otherness of nature itself, while fishing in a darkening river; with a sudden sense of alien threat he feels 'the hair rise/as something touched my boot' ('The River'). The sense of not belonging, of 'trespass' as Andrew Young terms it in 'The Fear', seems in many ways the obverse of wonder; both arise from an acute sense of separateness from the environment, from the impossibility of ever being part of it.

John Milton created one of the classic frightening landscapes – his amazingly powerful description of hell in *Paradise Lost* – by perverting all the qualities then thought to make the ideal view. His imaginary world owes as much to the increasing sophistication of contemporary descriptions of actual landscapes – with their control of depth and perspective – as to Milton's own extraordinary control of language.

James Thomson's cityscape, drawing on his contemporary Glasgow as inspiration, also has a distinct chthonic quality:

> never there
> Can come the lucid morning's fragrant breath
> After the dewy dawning's cold grey air;
> The moon and stars may shine with scorn or pity;
> The sun has never visited that city
> For it dissolveth in the daylight fair.

'The City of Dreadful Night'

Human perversion of the landscape reaches its ultimate extremes in war. The changed landscapes left behind – appalling in their bloody stillness or their almost-normality – manifest the destructive horror of war, and symbolise human fear of war itself:

The gentle slopes are green to remind you
of South English places, only far wider and flatter spread and
grooved and harrowed criss-cross whitely and the disturbed
subsoil heaped up albescent.

David Jones, 'In Parenthesis'

★   ★   ★

If a single quality can be abstracted from the poems in this book it is perhaps that of inclusiveness – a refusal to separate environments into neat categories, to divide living and non-living, to separate the 'objective self' from
the environment. This is surely an apt quality, being after all one of the
guiding ecological principles. In *The Orphic Voice* literary critic Elizabeth
Sewell tackles the relationship between poetry and biology, ecology's original 'parent' discipline. She sees an essential connection between the two:

Biology has mistaken its mythology. It needs poetry rather than
mathematics or language-as-science to think with; not an exclusive
but an inclusive mythology to match the principle of inclusion
inherent in all of its living and organic and synthetic subject matter.
Its failure [so to do] has imprisoned us in old habits of thought which
try to restrict the world to their narrowness.

The Orphic Voice, 1960

In the last ten years, many people have derived great optimism from the
fact that some of the challenges to these 'narrow habits of thought' have
actually come from within science itself. 'New science' theories such as
David Bohm's process physics and chaos theory in mathematics have revo-
lutionised scientific thinking. The mechanistic equations which formed the
basis of classical science and were assumed to be adequate to explain the
world around us, are no longer sufficient. Chaos, an incredibly complex
matrix of interpenetrating connections in which a small effect may lead to a
large one, may be a much truer reflection of the world around us.
Environmental and biological systems in particular – weather patterns, population, ecological patterns – are likely to be governed by nonlinear chaotic
relationships. It was from the study of weather patterns that chaos theory
first emerged, with the so-called 'butterfly effect', in which the flapping of

the wings of a butterfly causes tiny air movements that are transmitted and amplified until they cause a major change in the weather later, thousands of miles away.

Scientist James Lovelock's Gaia hypothesis incorporates all supposedly non-living things – oceans, rivers, soil, atmosphere – into one vastly complex self-regulating organism: Gaia, the earth, the whole of which is 'alive like a tree'. Poets, meanwhile, continue to challenge us all to see this 'aliveness', which has always been the wellspring of poetic interpretation of the world about us. At the end of the eighteenth century the poet Friedrich Hölderlin pleaded for the unity of reason with poetry and myth as the only true route to the understanding of the earth:

> Cold lying mouths; how dare you name the gods!
> Reason's your line. You never gave belief
> To Helios, the Thunderer, the Sea-God.
> The earth is dead – and shall we thank you for it?

'Die Scheinheiligen Dichter'

Sara Dunn, 1991

Celebration

'So I shake with joy'

Kathleen Raine

'THE VERY LEAVES OF THE ACACIA-TREE ARE LONDON'

The very leaves of the acacia-tree are London;
London tap-water fills out the fuchsia buds in the back garden,
Blackbirds pull London worms out of the sour soil,
The woodlice, centipedes, eat London, the wasps even.
London air through stomata of myriad leaves
and million lungs of London breathes.
Chlorophyll and haemoglobin do what life can
To purify, to return this great explosion
To sanity of leaf and wing.
Gradual and gentle the growth of London Pride,
And sparrows are free of all the time in the world:
Less than a window-pane between.

Nazim Hikmet

FABLE OF FABLES

Resting by the water-side
the plane tree and I.
Our reflections are thrown on the water
the plane tree's and mine.
The sparkle of the water hits us
the plane tree and me.

Resting by the water-side
the plane tree, I and the cat.
Our reflections are thrown on the water
the plane tree's, mine and the cat's.
The sparkle of the water hits us
the plane tree, me and the cat.

Resting by the water-side
the plane tree I, the cat and the sun.
Our reflections are thrown on the water
the plane tree's, mine, the cat's, and the sun's.
The sparkle of the water hits us
the plane tree, me, the cat and the sun.

Resting by the water-side
the plane tree, I, the cat, the sun and our life.
Our reflections are thrown on the water
the plane tree's, mine and the cat's, the sun's and our life's.
The sparkle of the water hits us
the plane tree, me, the cat, the sun and our life.

Resting by the water-side.
First the cat will go
its reflection will be lost on the water.
Then I will go
my reflection will be lost on the water.
Then the plane tree will go
Its reflection will be lost on the water.
Then the water will go
the sun will remain
then it will go too.

Resting by the water-side
the plane tree, I, the cat, the sun and our life.
The water is cool
the plane tree is huge
I am writing a poem
the sun is warm
it's great to be alive.
The sparkle of the water hits us
the plane tree, me, the cat, the sun, our life.

Translated by Richard McKane

Langston Hughes

DREAM VARIATION

To fling my arms wide
In some place of the sun,
To whirl and to dance
Till the white day is done.
Then rest at cool evening
Beneath a tall tree
While night comes on gently,
   Dark like me –
That is my dream!

To fling my arms wide
In the face of the sun,
Dance! Whirl! Whirl!
Till the quick day is done.
Rest at pale evening . . .
A tall, slim tree . . .
Night coming tenderly
   Black like me.

Uvavnuk (*Iglulik Eskimo woman*)

MOVED

The great sea stirs me.
The great sea sets me adrift,
it sways me like the weed
on a river-stone.

The sky's height stirs me.
The strong wind blows through my mind.
It carries me with it,
so I shake with joy.

Translated by Tom Lowenstein

Walt Whitman

From SONG OF MYSELF

I believe a leaf of grass is no less than the journey-work of
    the stars,
And the pismire is equally perfect, and a grain of sand, and the
    egg of the wren,
And the tree-toad is a chef-d'oeuvre for the highest,
And the running blackberry would adorn the parlors of
    heaven,
And the narrowest hinge in my hand puts to scorn all
    machinery,

And the cow crunching with depress'd head surpasses any
    statue,
And a mouse is miracle enough to stagger sextillions of
    infidels.

I find I incorporate gneiss, coal, long-threaded moss, fruits,
    grains, esculent roots,
And am stucco'd with quadrupeds and birds all over,
And have distanced what is behind me for good reasons,
But call any thing back again when I desire it.

In vain the speeding or shyness,
In vain the plutonic rocks send their old heat against my
    approach,
In vain the mastodon retreats beneath its own powder'd
    bones,
In vain objects stand leagues off and assume manifold shapes,
In vain the ocean setting in hollows and the great monsters
    lying low,
In vain the buzzard houses herself with the sky,
In vain the snake slides through the creepers and logs,
In vain the elk takes to the inner passes of the woods,
In vain the razor-bill'd auk sails far north to Labrador,
I follow quickly, I ascend to the nest in the fissure of the
    cliff.

Hugh MacDiarmid

From SCOTTISH SCENE

He heard the corn-buntin' cry 'Guid-night'
And the lark 'Guid-mornin',' and kent by sight
And call-note the Osprey and the Erne,
The Blue-Hawk and the Merlin and the Kite,
The Honey Buzzard and the Snowy Owl,
The Ring Ouzel, the Black Cap, the Wood Wren,
The Mealy Redpole, the Purple Heron, the Avocet,
The Gadwell, the Shoveller, and the Raven.

He loved the haill o' the countryside
And kent it as nae ither man ever kent
The coast rocks wi' the wild seas lashin' their feet,
And the myriads o' seabirds that cam' and went,
Kittywake, guillemot, razor-bill, puffin,
Whiles darkenin' the air wi' their multitudes,
Wheelin' in endless and varyin' airts
– He kent them singly in a' their moods.

Fishin'-boats shoot oot frae the rocky clefts
In which the harbours are formed – below
The Gardenstown boats and Crovie's to the right,
The fleets frae Fraserburgh eastward show,
Westward the boats frae Macduff and Banff,
Whitehills, Portsoy, Findochtie, the Buckies
– He wishes he was aboard each at aince
Kaimin' their nets to see that his luck is!

Far owre the Moray firth the Caithness mountains
Are clearly picked oot 'gainst the evenin' sky.
The hills o' Morven and the Maiden's Pap
A' stand within the scope o' his eye,
And every slope o' hard grauwacke he kens,
The Reid Hill o' Penman, the Bin Hill o' Cullen,
The Dens o' Aberdour, Auchmeddie, and Troup
– Shairly a land nae man can be dull in!

Boris Pasternak

STEPPE

How good it was then to go out into quietness!
The steppe's boundless seascape flows to the sky.
The feather grass sighs, ants rustle in it,
And the keening mosquito floats by.

Haystacks have lined themselves up with clouds,
The cones of volcanoes cooling to grey,
The boundless steppe has grown silent and damp;
It rocks you, buffets you, bears you away.

Mist has surrounded us here like the sea,
Burs clutching our stockings, and how good today
To wander the steppe like the shore of the sea;
It rocks you, buffets you, bears you away.

Is that not a haystack? Who knows?
Is that not our rick coming closer? Yes. Found!
The very one, Rick, mist, and steppe,
Rick, mist, and steppe all round.

Off to the right runs the Milky Way
To Kerch, like a highroad the cattle pound
To dust. It will take your breath away
Behind the huts: such distances all round.

The mist soporific, the grass like honey,
The Milky Way in feather grass drowned.
The mist will disperse and the night will embrace
The haystack and steppe all round.

Crepuscular midnight stands by the road,
Where the stars have spilled from its purse.
You cannot go over the road past the fence
Without trampling the universe.

When did the stars ever grow so low
And midnight fall to the feather-grassed ground
And muslin mist catch alight and cling,
Thirst for the grand finale to sound?

Let the steppe judge between us and night decide
When and when not: in the Beginning
Did Ants Creep on Grass, did Mosquitoes Keen,
Did Bur Clutch at Stocking?

Shut your eyes, darling, or you will be blinded!
The steppe is tonight as before the Fall:
All lapped in peace, all like a parachute,
A rearing vision, all.

Henry Thoreau

LOW-ANCHORED CLOUD

Low-anchored cloud,
Newfoundland air,
Fountain-head and source of rivers,
Dew-cloth, dream drapery,
And napkin spread by fays;
Drifting meadow of the air,
Where bloom the daisied banks and violets,
And in whose fenny labyrinth
The bittern booms and heron wades;
Spirit of lakes and seas and rivers,
Bear only perfumes and the scent
Of healing herbs to just men's fields!

Geoffrey Chaucer

From THE PARLIAMENT OF FOWLS

A gardyn saw I ful of blosmy bowes
Upon a ryver, in a grene mede,
There as swetnesse everemore inow is,
With floures white, blewe, yelwe, and rede,
And colde welle-stremes, nothyng dede,
That swymmen ful of smale fishes lighte,
With fynnes rede and skales sylver bryghte.

On every bow the bryddes herde I synge,   *birds*
With voys of aungel in here armonye;   *their*
Some besyede hem here bryddes forth to brynge;
The litel conyes to here pley gonne hye;   *made haste*
And ferther al aboute I gan aspye
The dredful ro, the buk, the hert and hynde,   *timid*
Squyrels, and bestes smale of gentil kynde.

Of instruments of strenges in acord
Herde I so pleye a ravyshyng swetnesse,
That God, that makere is of al and lord,
Ne herde nevere beter, as I gesse.
Therwith a wynd, unnethe it myghte be lesse,   *hardly*
Made in the leves grene a noyse softe
Acordaunt to the foules song alofte.   *in harmony with*

Th'air of that place so attempre was   *mild*
That nevere was ther grevaunce of hot ne cold;
There wex ek every holsom spice and gras;
No man may there waxe sek ne old;   *also grew*
Yet was there joye more a thousandfold
Than man can telle; ne nevere wolde it nyghte,
But ay cler day to any manes syghte.

'Abd Allah ibn al-Simak

THE GARDEN

The garden of green hillocks
dresses up for visitors
in the most beautiful colors

as if a young woman's dowry
were spread out
glittering with gold necklaces

or as if someone had poured out
censers of musk powder
mixed with the purest aromatic oils.

Birds trill on the branches
like singing girls
bending over their lutes

and water falls continuously
like neckchains
of silver and pearls.

These are splendors of such perfection
they call to mind
the beauty of absolute certainty,
the radiance of faith.

Translated by Cola Franzen

Alden Nowlan

SACRAMENT

God, I have sought you as a fox seeks chickens,
curbing my hunger with cunning.
The times I have tasted your flesh
there was no bread and wine between us,
only night and the wind beating the grass.

Margaret Walker

MY MISSISSIPPI SPRING

My heart warms under snow;
flowers with forsythia,
japonica blooms, flowering quince,
bridal wreath, blood root and violet;
yellow running jasmin vine,
cape jessamine and saucer magnolias:
tulip-shaped, scenting lemon musk upon the air.
My Mississippi Spring –
my warm loving heart a-fire
with early greening leaves,
dogwood branches laced against the sky;
wild forest nature paths
heralding Resurrection
over and over again
Easter morning of our living
every Mississippi Spring!

Denise Levertov

SPRING IN THE LOWLANDS

Shout into leaping wind
alone by spring lakes
On muddy paths, yellow grass
stamp, laugh; no one
to hear.

The water, water, dazzles;
                              dark winds
pluck its feathers
        splash the hissing reeds.
Birches lean on the air.

Lean into solitude
you whose joy is a kite
now dragged in dirt, now
breaking the ritual of sky.

Olga Broumas

FOR ROBBIE MOORE

The things that give such pleasure to the eye, a clothesline
stretched from porch to pine, sixth in a row, eight old
loyal increments I caretake, squat among. The wood splits

easy, Tamarack, the axe slowmotion penetrates, cleaves
to the block. The cat is friendly, eats her mice and birds
under the bed. Coyote barks, the old black lab barks back. Dawn

and the wind bows slowly to the shield of trees. Northwest, Southeast.
It's quiet here, windows uncurtained you can see horizon from
horizon. Sunset and moonrise balancebeam, the house at sea. The hills,

benign and magnified, multiply unendangered, field after sandy field.
How beautiful, the farmgirl held the slide of dunes and the Pacific
to the sky, *how beautiful*, she said, *blue fields*. Fields

choking with stars, the beautiful black silent fields each night they mine
me rib by rib and find the bitter almond cloves they fill with honey.

Praxilla

'MOST BEAUTIFUL OF THINGS'

Most beautiful of things I leave is sunlight;
then come glazing stars and the moon's face;
then ripe cucumbers and apples and pears.

Gerard Manley Hopkins

'REPEAT THAT, REPEAT'

Repeat that, repeat,
Cuckoo, bird, and open ear wells, heart-springs, delight-
    fully sweet,
With a ballad, with a ballad, a rebound
Off trundled timber and scoops of the hillside ground,
    hollow hollow hollow ground:
The whole landscape flushes on a sudden at a sound.

John Clare

PLEASANT SOUNDS

The rustling of leaves under the feet in woods and under hedges;
The crumping of cat-ice and snow down wood-rides, narrow
    lanes, and every street causeway;
Rustling through a wood or rather rushing, while the wind
    halloos in the oak-top like thunder;
The rustle of birds' wings startled from their nests or flying
    unseen into the bushes;
The whizzing of larger birds overhead in a wood, such as crows,
    puddocks, buzzards;
The trample of robins and woodlarks on the brown leaves, and
    the patter of squirrels on the green moss;
The fall of an acorn on the ground, the pattering of nuts on the
    hazel branches as they fall from ripeness;
The flirt of the groundlark's wing from the stubbles – how
    sweet such pictures on dewy mornings, when the dew
    flashes from its brown feathers!

William Cowper

From THE TASK, BOOK I

Nor rural sights alone, but rural sounds,
Exhilarate the spirit, and restore
The tone of languid Nature. Mighty winds,
That sweep the skirt of some far-spreading wood
Of ancient growth, make music not unlike
The dash of ocean on his winding shore,
And lull the spirit while they fill the mind;
Unnumber'd branches waving in the blast,
And all their leaves fast flutt'ring, all at once.
Nor less composure waits upon the roar
Of distant floods, or on the softer voice
Of neighb'ring fountain, or of rills that slip
Through the cleft rock, and, chiming as they fall
Upon loose pebbles, lose themselves at length
In matted grass, that with a livelier green
Betrays the secret of their silent course.
Nature inanimate employs sweet sounds,
But animated nature sweeter still,
To sooth and satisfy the human ear.
Ten thousand warblers cheer the day, and one
The live-long night: nor these alone, whose notes
Nice finger'd art must emulate in vain,
But cawing rooks, and kites that swim sublime
In still repeated circles, screaming loud,
The jay, the pie and ev'n the boding owl
That hails the rising moon, have charms for me.
Sounds inharmonious in themselves and harsh,
Yet heard in scenes where peace for ever reigns,
And only there, please highly for their sake.

Percy Bysshe Shelley

From EPIPSYCHIDION

It is an isle under Ionian skies
Beautiful as a wreck of Paradise,
And, for the harbours are not safe and good,
This land would have remained a solitude
But for some pastoral people native there,
Who from the Elysian, clear, and golden air
Draw the last spirit of the age of gold,
Simple and spirited; innocent and bold.
The blue Aegean girds this chosen home,
With ever-changing sound and light and foam,
Kissing the sifted sands, and caverns hoar;
And all the winds wandering along the shore
Undulate with the undulating tide:
There are thick woods where sylvan forms abide;
And many a fountain, rivulet, and pond,
As clear as elemental diamond,
Or serene morning air; and far beyond,
The mossy tracks made by the goats and deer
(Which the rough shepherd treads but once a year)
Pierce into glades, caverns, and bowers, and halls
Built round with ivy, which the waterfalls
Illumining, with sound that never fails
Accompany the noonday nightingales;
And all the place is peopled with sweet airs;
The light clear element which the isle wears
Is heavy with the scent of lemon-flowers,
Which floats like mist laden with unseen showers,
And falls upon the eyelids like faint sleep;
And from the moss violets and jonquils peep,
And dart their arrowy odour through the brain
Till you might faint with that delicious pain.
And every motion, odour, beam, and tone,
With that deep music is in unison:
Which is a soul within the soul – they seem
Like echoes of an antenatal dream. –
It is an isle 'twixt Heaven, Air, Earth, and Sea,

Cradled, and hung in clear tranquillity;
Bright as that wandering Eden Lucifer,
Washed by the soft blue Oceans of young air.
It is a favoured place. Famine or Blight,
Pestilence, War and Earthquake, never light
Upon its mountain-peaks; blind vultures, they
Sail onward far upon their fatal way:
The wingèd storms, chanting their thunder-psalm
To other lands, leave azure chasms of calm
Over this isle, or weep themselves in dew,
From which its fields and woods ever renew
Their green and golden immortality.

Sappho

'LEAVE KRETE AND COME TO THIS HOLY TEMPLE'

Leave Krete and come to this holy temple
where the graceful grove of apple trees
circles an altar smoking with frank-
incense.

Here roses leave shadows on the ground
and cold springs babble through apple branches
where shuddering leaves pour down profound sleep.

In our meadows where horses graze
and wild flowers of spring blossom,
anise shoots fill the air with a-
roma.

And here, Aphrodite, pour
heavenly nectar into gold cups
and fill them gracefully with sudden joy.

Translated by Willis Barnstone

Michael Drayton

From POLY-OLBION, THE FIRST SONG

Of Albions glorious Ile the wonders whilst I write,
The sundry varying soyles, the pleasures infinite
(Where heate kills not the cold, nor cold expells the
    heat,
The calmes too mildly small, nor winds too roughly
    great,
Nor night doth hinder day, nor day the night doth
    wrong,
The summer not too short, the winter not too long)
What helpe shall I invoke to ayde my Muse the while?
    Thou genius of the place (this most renowned ile)
Which livedst long before the all-earth-drowning
    flood,
Whilst yet the world did swarme with her gigantick
    brood;
Goe thou before me still thy circling shores about,
And in this wandring maze helpe to conduct me out:
Direct my course so right, as with thy hand to showe
Which way thy forrests range, which way thy rivers
    flowe;
Wise genius, by thy helpe that so I may discry
How thy faire mountaines stand, and how thy
    vallyes lie;
From those cleere pearlie cleeves which see the
    mornings pride,
And check the surlie impes of Neptune when they
    chide,
Unto the big-swolne waves in the Iberian streame,
Where Titan still unyokes his fiery-hoofed teame,
And oft his flaming locks in lushious nectar steepes,
When from Olympus top he plungeth in the deepes:
That from th'Armorick sands, on surging Neptunes
    leas
Through the Hibernick Gulfe (those rough Vergivian
    seas)
My verse with wings of skill may flie a loftie gate,
As Amphitrilé clips this iland fortunate,
Till through the sleepy maine to Thuly I have gone,

As Amphitrite clips this iland fortunate,
Till through the sleepy maine to Thuly I have gone,
And seene the frozen iles, the cold Ducalidon,
Amongst whose iron rockes grym Saturne yet
    remaines
Bound in those gloomie caves with adamantine
    chaines.

Wendy Rose

MOUNT SAINT HELEN'S/LOOWIT:
AN INDIAN WOMAN'S SONG
March 30, 1980

Having unbuckled themselves
from their airline seats
the passengers found each
a tiny window on the left side
of the jet and stared like voyeurs
into the bellows of her throat,
watched the convulsions shaking her
till she raged
and waved her round hands
in the sky.

Some gave up easily,
said 'She looks just like
any mountain covered with snow
as winter eases
into spring.' Others
closed their eyes,
and waited for supper.
I applauded
called for an encore,
amd wished to soar
around her in an honoring dance
because in her labor
she holds
the planet in place.

In five minutes
we had flown completely by,
leaving her eastern slope blackened
and eyelids fluttering
as one slowly waking.

Southeast
Mazama nods
and waits.

Friedrich Hölderlin

'YOU FIRMLY BUILT ALPS!'

You firmly built alps!
That

And you mildly glancing mountains,
Where over the bushy slope
The Black Forest rushes
And the fir tree's curl
Pours down pleasing odours
And the Neckar

and the Danube!

In summer the garden wafts
About a loving fever,
And the village's lindens, and where
The black poplar blossoms
And the white mulberry
On a holy pasture,

And

You good cities!
Not misshapen, mingled with
The enemy, powerless

Which
All at once it goes away
And does not see death.
But when

And Stuttgart, where
A momentary one I might be allowed
To lie buried, at the place
Where the road
Bends, and
     around the Weinstaig
And the city's hubbub meets
Itself once more down below on the level sward
Quietly sounding among the apple trees

Of Tübingen   where
And in day's full   glare
Lightning flashes fall
And the Spitzberg, resounding, yields Roman lore
And pleasing odour

And Thill's valley, which

Translated by Michael Hamburger

William Wordsworth

COMPOSED UPON WESTMINSTER BRIDGE
September 3, 1802

Earth has not anything to show more fair:
Dull would he be of soul who could pass by
A sight so touching in its majesty:
This City now doth, like a garment, wear
The beauty of the morning; silent, bare,
Ships, towers, domes, theatres, and temples lie
Open unto the fields, and to the sky;
All bright and glittering in the smokeless air.
Never did sun more beautifully steep
In his first splendour, valley, rock, or hill;
Ne'er saw I, never felt, a calm so deep!
The river glideth at his own sweet will:
Dear God! the very houses seem asleep;
And all that mighty heart is lying still!

Anne Wilson

From TEISA: A DESCRIPTIVE POEM OF THE RIVER TEES, ITS TOWNS AND ANTIQUITIES
[In Praise of Drainage]

Yonder behold a little purling rill,
Sweet flowing down the green, enamelled hill:
This aqueduct proceeds from Morrit's drains,
And well compensates his ingenious pains.
The rotten ground, which trembled as we trod,
Is now released from the exuberant load
Of chilly waters, that the grass deprive
Of its nutritious particles, and drive,
With moist, diluting qualities, away
The salts impregnating the foodful hay.
Where the dejected sheep all bleating stood,
Benumbed with chilly damps, and starved for food,
Behold firm land appear, with wholesome grass;
The cattle's looks proclaim it as we pass;

Death, which so oft in tainted rots appeared,
Is by the farmer now no longer feared.

This plan would each landholder but pursue,
England a paradise we then might view:
Not then would her own sons, like exiles, seek
More lands to till beyond the foaming deep.
Lovers of agriculture all might here
Employment find throughout the circling year,
Since convenient are all seasons found
To drain off waters from the spongy ground.

The model of the drains prepare to sing,
O Sylvan Muse! Find out the hidden spring
Where bubbling waters rise, then with a spade
Let a broad trench, three feet in depth, be made;
Observe that with descent your conduit run,
Whether to the rising or the setting sun;
Let it in breadth about a foot extend,
And with a wall you must its sides defend;
This wall in height at least must be a foot,
And over the canal be sure to put
Large shelvy stones – the wall will them sustain;
With ling or straw then cover it again;
And careful stop each little hole or chink,
Lest through these the mouldering earth should sink,
Which oft the water's rapid course impedes.
But when th' earth is fixed, there no longer needs
Aught, save the stones, to bear it off the rills,
Which now the springing water quickly fills;
Every lesser duct must have its course
Into a larger one, which adds its force
To drive redundant fluids off the land,
Which, like a deluge, once were used to stand:
When this is done, it only now remains
With their own earth to cover up the drains . . .

Abraham Cowley

From A PARAPHRASE UPON THE TENTH EPISTLE
OF THE FIRST BOOK OF HORACE
Horace to Fuscus Aristius

Health from the lover of the country, me,
Health to the lover of the city, thee;
A difference in our souls, this only proves;
In all things else, we agree like married doves.
But the warm nest and crowded dove-house thou
Dost like; I loosely fly from bough to bough,
And rivers drink, and all the shining day,
Upon fair trees or mossy rocks, I play;
In fine, I live and reign, when I retire
From all that you equal with heaven admire.
Like one at last from the priest's service fled,
Loathing the honied cakes, I long for bread.
Would I a house for happiness erect,
Nature alone should be the architect,
She'd build it more convenient, than great,
And, doubtless, in the country choose her seat.
Is there a place doth better helps supply,
Against the wounds of winter's cruelty?
Is there an air, that gentlier does assuage
The mad celestial dog's, or lion's rage?
Is it not there that sleep (and only there)
Nor noise without, nor cares within, does fear?
Does art through pipes a purer water bring,
Than that, which nature strains into a spring?
Can all your tap'stries, or your pictures, show
More beauties, than in herbs and flowers do grow?
Fountains and trees our wearied pride do please,
Even in the midst of gilded palaces.
And in your towns, that prospect gives delight,
Which opens round the country to our sight.
Men to the good, from which they rashly fly,
Return at last; and their wild luxury
Does but in vain with those true joys contend,
Which nature did to mankind recommend.

Gerard Manley Hopkins

INVERSNAID

This darksome burn, horseback brown,
His rollrock highroad roaring down,
In coop and in comb the fleece of his foam
Flutes and low to the lake falls home.

A windpuff-bonnet of fáwn-fróth
Turns and twindles over the broth
Of a pool so pitchblack, féll-frówning,
It rounds and rounds Despair to drowning.

Degged with dew, dappled with dew
Are the groins of the braes that the brook treads through,
Wiry heathpacks, flitches of fern,
And the beadbonny ash that sits over the burn.

What would the world be, once bereft
Of wet and of wildness? Let them be left,
O let them be left, wildness and wet;
Long live the weeds and the wilderness yet.

James Thomson

From THE SEASONS

WINTER

   To thy loved haunt return, my happy Muse:
For now, behold, the joyous winter days,
Frosty, succeed; and through the blue serene,
For sight too fine, the ethereal nitre flies;
Killing infectious damps, and the spent air
Storing afresh with elemental life.
Close crowds the shining atmosphere; and binds
Our strengthen'd bodies in its cold embrace,
Constringent; feeds, and animates our blood;
Refines our spirits, through the new-strung nerves,

In swifter sallies darting to the brain;
Where sits the soul, intense, collected, cool.
Bright as the skies, and as the season keen.
All Nature feels the renovating force
Of Winter, only to the thoughtless eye
In ruin seen. The frost-concocted glebe
Draws in abundant vegetable soul,
And gathers vigour for the coming year,
A stronger glow sits on the lively cheek
Of ruddy fire: and luculent along
The purer rivers flow; their sullen deeps
Transparent, open to the shepherd's gaze,
And murmur hoarser at the fixing frost.

Basho

'YEARS END'

Year's end,
all corners
of this floating world, swept.

W.H. Davies

A BRIGHT DAY

My windows now are giant drops of dew
  The common stones are dancing in my eyes;
The light is winged, and panting, and the world
  Is fluttering with a little fall or rise.

See, while they shoot the sun with singing Larks,
  How those broad meadows sparkle and rejoice!
Where can the Cuckoo hide in all this light,
  And still remain unseen, and but a voice?

Shall I be mean, when all this light is mine?
  Is anything unworthy of its place?
Call for the rat, and let him share my joy,
  And sit beside me here, to wash his face.

Loss

'Lament for all that is purple like dusk'

Gerard Manley Hopkins

BINSEY POPLARS
felled 1879

My aspens dear, whose airy cages quelled,
Quelled or quenched in leaves the leaping sun,
All felled, felled, are all felled;
   Of a fresh and following folded rank
      Not spared, not one
      That dandled a sandalled
    Shadow that swam or sank
On meadow and river and wind-wandering weed-winding
   bank.

  O if we knew what we do
      When we delve or hew—
   Hack and rack the growing green!
     Since country is so tender
  To touch, her being só slender,
  That, like this sleek and seeing ball
  But a prick will make no eye at all,
  Where we, even where we mean
      To mend her we end her,
    When we hew or delve:
After-comers cannot guess the beauty been.
  Ten or twelve, only ten or twelve
   Strokes of havoc únselve
    The sweet especial scene,
  Rural scene, a rural scene,
  Sweet especial rural scene.

Cassiano Ricardo

THE SONG OF THE WILD DOVE

Deep within the backlands I walked along the road,
the coffee plantation was far away.
It was then I heard your song
sounding like the endless sobbing of distance . . .

The longing for all that is tall like palm trees.
The yearning for all that is long like rivers . . .
The lament for all that is purple like dusk . . .
The weeping of all that weeps because it is far away . . .
        very far away.

Translated by Jean R. Longland

Dorothy Parker

TEMPS PERDU

I never may turn the loop of a road
    Where sudden, ahead, the sea is lying,
But my heart drags down with an ancient load –
    My heart, that a second before was flying.

I never behold the quivering rain –
    And sweeter the rain than a lover to me –
But my heart is wild in my breast with pain;
    My heart, that was tapping contentedly.

There's never a rose spreads a new at my door
    Nor a strange bird crosses the moon at night
But I know I have known its beauty before,
    And a terrible sorrow along with the sight.

The look of a laurel tree birthed for May
    Or a sycamore bared for a new November
Is as old and as sad as my furtherest day –
    What is it, what is it, I almost remember?

Ahmad 'Abd al-Mu'tí Hijází

CAPTION TO A LANDSCAPE

A sun setting on a wintry horizon,
A red sun,
Leaden clouds,
Pierced by bundles of light,
And me, a peasant child,
Overwhelmed by night.

Our car was devouring the asphalt thread,
Climbing from our village to the city,
And I wished to hurl myself
Onto the moist verdure.

A sun setting on a wintry horizon,
A magic castle,
A gate of light
Opening on a time of legend,
The palm of a hand stained with henna,
A peacock ascending through the heavens,
Its rainbow tail spread out.

In the past, when the sun was setting,
God would appear to me
As a gardener
Walking down the pink horizon
And scattering water
Over the verdant world.
The picture is still clear
But the child who drew it
Has been crushed by the passage of days.

Janice Gould

DISPOSSESSED

I remember in October
driving to the mountains,
the kids piled in the back of the pick-up,
tucked under sleeping bags and blankets.
We drank coffee from a thermos
spiked with a slug of brandy.
There was already snow
on the north face of the ridges,
a storm chased flocks of migrant birds south.
We were headed for Maidu country.
Maples had yellow leaves,
a clear, cold breeze
blew through the canyon,
there was frost on the meadows in the morning,
woodsmoke and mist in the evening.
At the new tavern
built on the homestead
where my mom once lived,
two Indian girls drank beer
and played pool with some white guys.
They looked at me strangely
when we came in,
and what should seem familiar
was foreign and strained.
This is not my land anymore.
The creek where Mama played,
the graveyard up the hill
that lies beneath the hum
of massive power lines,
the cabin with its spirit children –
these things are not mine.

Jorge Carrera Andrade

BIOGRAPHY FOR THE USE OF THE BIRDS

I was born in the century of the death of the rose
when the motor had already driven out the angels.
Quito watched the last stagecoach roll,
and at its passing the trees ran by in good order,
and the hedges and houses of the new parishes,
on the threshold of the country
where slow cows were ruminating the silence
and the wind spurred its swift horses.

My mother, clothed in the setting sun,
put away her youth in a deep guitar,
and only on certain evenings would she show it to her
        children
sheathed in music, light and words.
I loved the water-writing of the rain,
the yellow gnats from the apple tree,
and the toads that would sound from time to time
their bulging wooden bells.

The great sail of the air manoeuvred endlessly.
The mountain range was a shoreline of the sky.
The storm would come and at the roll of its drum
its drenched regiments would charge;
but then the sun with its golden patrols
would bring back translucent peace to the fields.

I would watch men clasp the barley,
horsemen sink into the sky,
and the wagons filled with lowing oxen
go down to the coast fragrant with mangoes.

The valley was there with its farms
where dawn touched off its trickle of roosters,
and westward was the land where the sugarcane
rippled its peaceful banner, and the cacao
held close in a coffer its secret fortune,
and the pineapple girded on its fragrant cuirasse,
the naked banana its tunic of silk.

All has gone now, in sequent waves,
like the futile cyphers of the foam.
The years go leisurely entangling their lichens,
and memory is scarcely a water-lily
showing on the surface timidly
its drowned face.
The guitar is only a coffin for songs,
and the head-wounded cock laments.
All the angels of the earth have emigrated,
even the dark angel of the cacao tree.

Translated by Donald Devenish Walsh

Margaret Walker

OCTOBER JOURNEY

Traveller take heed for journeys undertaken in the dark of
    the year.
Go in the bright blaze of Autumn's equinox.
Carry protection against ravages of a sun-robber, a vandal,
    a thief.
Cross no bright expanse of water in the full of the
    moon.
Choose no dangerous summer nights;
no heavy tempting hours of spring;
October journeys are safest, brightest, and best.

I want to tell you what hills are like in October
when colors gush down mountainsides
and little streams are freighted with a caravan of leaves,
I want to tell you how they blush and turn in fiery shame
    and joy,
how their love burns with flames consuming and terrible
until we wake one morning and woods are like a smoldering
    plain—
a glowing cauldron full of jewelled fire;
the emerald earth a dragon's eye
the poplars drenched with yellow light
and dogwoods blazing bloody red.
Travelling southward earth changes from gray rock to green
    velvet.
Earth changes to red clay
with green grass growing brightly
with saffron skies of evening setting dully
with muddy rivers moving sluggishly.

In the early spring when the peach tree blooms
wearing a veil like a lavender haze
and the pear and plum in their bridal hair
gently snow their petals on earth's grassy bosom below
then the soughing breeze is soothing
and the world seems bathed in tenderness,
but in October
blossoms have long since fallen.
A few red apples hang on leafless boughs;
wind whips bushes briskly.
And where a blue stream sings cautiously
a barren land feeds hungrily.

An evil moon bleeds drops of death.
The earth burns brown.
Grass shrivels and dries to a yellowish mass.
Earth wears a dun-colored dress
like an old woman wooing the sun to be her lover,
be her sweetheart and her husband bound in one.
Farmers heap hay in stacks and bind corn in shocks
against the biting breath of frost.

The train wheels hum, 'I am going home, I am going home
I am moving toward the South.'
Soon cypress swamps and muskrat marshes
and black fields touched with cotton will appear.
I dream again of my childhood land
of a neighbor's yard with a redbud tree
the smell of pine for turpentine
an Easter dress, a Christmas eve
and winding roads from the top of a hill.
A music sings within my flesh
I feel the pulse within my throat
my heart fills up with hungry fear
while hills and flatlands stark and staring
before my dark eyes sad and haunting
appear and disappear.

Then when I touch this land again
the promise of a sun-lit hour dies.
The greenness of an apple seems
to dry and rot before my eyes.
The sullen winter rains
are tears of grief I cannot shed.
The windless days are static lives.
The clock runs down
timeless and still.
The days and nights turn hours to years
and water in a gutter marks the circle of another world
hating, resentful, and afraid,
stagnant, and green, and full of slimy things.

Anon [Medieval Latin]

From THE CAMBRIDGE SONGS

This *planctus* (lament) (ca. 1000) is the
best-known surviving woman's lament from the
Latin Middle Ages.

Wind is thin,
sun warm,
the earth overflows
with good things.

Spring is purple
jewelry;
flowers on the ground,
green in the forest.

Quadrupeds shine
and wander. Birds
nest. On blossoming
branches they cry joy!

My eyes see, my ears
hear so much, and
I am thrilled.
Yet I swallow sighs.

Sitting here alone,
I turn pale. When strong
enough to lift my head,
I hear and see nothing.

Spring, hear me.
Despite green woods,
blossoms and seed,
my spirit rots.

Translated by Willis Barnstone

Wendy Rose

LONG DIVISION: A TRIBAL HISTORY

Our skin loosely lies
across grass borders;
stones loading up
are loaded down with placement sticks,
a great tearing
and appearance of holes.
We are bought and divided
into clay pots; we die
on granite scaffolding
on the shape of the Sierras
and lie down with lips open
thrusting songs on the world.
Who are we and do we
still live? The doctor,
asleep, says no.
So outside of eternity
we struggle until our blood
has spread off our bodies
and frayed the sunset edges.
It's our blood that gives you
those southwestern skies.
Year after year we give,
harpooned with hope, only to fall
bouncing through the canyons,
our sings decreasing
with distance.
I suckle coyotes
and grieve.

Claude McKay

THE TROPICS IN NEW YORK

Bananas ripe and green, and ginger root,
  Cocoa in pods and alligator pears,
And tangerines and mangoes and grape fruit,
  Fit for the highest prize at parish fairs.

Set in the window, bringing memories
  Of fruit-trees laden by low-singing rills,
And dewy dawns, and mystical blue skies
  In benediction over nun-like hills.

My eyes grew dim, and I could no more gaze;
  A wave of longing through my body swept,
And, hungry for the old familiar ways,
  I turned aside and bowed my head and wept.

John Clare

ENCLOSURE

Far spread the moory ground, a level scene
Bespread with rush and one eternal green,
That never felt the rage of blundering plough,
Though centuries wreathed spring blossoms on its brow.
Autumn met plains that stretched them far away
In unchecked shadows of green, brown, and grey.
Unbounded freedom ruled the wandering scene;
No fence of ownership crept in between
To hide the prospect from the gazing eye;
Its only bondage was the circling sky.
A mighty flat, undwarfed by bush and tree,
Spread its faint shadow of immensity,
And lost itself, which seemed to eke its bounds,
In the blue mist the horizon's edge surrounds.

Now this sweet vision of my boyish hours,
Free as spring clouds and wild as forest flowers,
Is faded all – a hope that blossomed free,
And hath been once as it no more shall be.
Enclosure came, and trampled on the grave
Of labour's rights, and left the poor a slave;
And memory's pride, ere want to wealth did bow,
Is both the shadow and the substance now.
The sheep and cows were free to range as then
Where change might prompt, nor felt the bonds of men.
Cows went and came with every morn and night
To the wild pasture as their common right;
And sheep, unfolded with the rising sun,
Heard the swains shout and felt their freedom won,
Tracked the red fallow field and heath and plain,
Or sought the brook to drink, and roamed again;
While the glad shepherd traced their tracks along,
Free as the lark and happy as her song.
But now all's fled and flats of many a dye
That seemed to lengthen with the following eye,
Moors losing from the sight, far, smooth, and blea,
Where swopt the plover in its pleasure free,
Are banished now with heaths once wild and gay
As poet's visions of life's early day.
Like mighty giants of their limbs bereft,
The skybound wastes in mangled garbs are left,
Fence meeting fence in owner's little bounds
Of field and meadow, large as garden-grounds,
In little parcels little minds to please,
With men and flocks imprisoned, ill at ease.
For with the poor scared freedom bade farewell,
And fortune-hunters totter where they fell;
They dreamed of riches in the rebel scheme
And find too truly that they did but dream.

Virgil

PASTORAL I

TITYRUS AND MELIBOEUS

The Argument

The occasion of the first Pastoral was this. When Augustus had settled himself in the Roman empire, that he might reward his veteran troops for their past service, he distributed among them all the lands that lay about Cremona and Mantua, turning out the right owners for having sided with his enemies. Virgil was a sufferer among the rest; who afterward recovered his estate by Maecenas' intercession, and, as an instance of his gratitude, composed the following Pastoral, where he sets out his own good fortune in the person of Tityrus, and the calamities of his Mantuan neighbours in the character of Meliboeus. (*J.D.*)

M. O fortunate old man! whose farm remains –
For you sufficient – and requites your pains;
Though rushes overspread the neighbouring plains,
Though here the marshy grounds approach your fields,
And there the soil a stony harvest yields.
Your teeming ewes shall no strange meadows try,
Nor fear a rot from tainted company.
Behold! yon bordering fence of sallow-trees
Is fraught with flowers; the flowers are fraught with
    bees:
The busy bees, with a soft murmuring strain,
Invite to gentle sleep the labouring swain.
While from the neighbouring rock, with rural songs,
The pruner's voice the pleasing dream prolongs,
Stock-doves and turtles tell their amorous pain,
And, from the lofty elms, of love complain.

★   ★   ★

But we must beg our bread in climes unknown,
Beneath the scorching or the freezing zone:
And some to far Oaxis shall be sold,
Or try the Libyan heat, or Scythian cold;
The rest among the Britons be confined:
A race of men from all the world disjoined.
O! must the wretched exiles ever mourn,
Nor, after length of rolling years, return?
Are we condemned by fate's unjust decree,
No more our houses and our homes to see?
Or shall we mount again the rural throne,
And rule the country kingdoms, once our own?
Did we for these barbarians plant and sow?
On these, on these, our happy fields bestow?
Good heaven! what dire effects from civil discord flow!
Now let me graff my pears and prune the vine;
The fruit is theirs, the labour only, mine.
Farewell, my pastures, my paternal stock,
My fruitful fields, and my more fruitful flock!
No more, my goats, shall I behold you climb
The steepy cliffs or crop the flowery thyme!
No more, extended in the grot below,
Shall see you browsing on the mountain's brow
The prickly shrubs, and after on the bare,
Lean down the deep abyss, and hang in air!
No more my sheep shall sip the morning dew;
No more my song shall please the rural crew:
Adieu, my tuneful pipe! and all the world, adieu!
   T. This night, at least, with me forget your care;
Chestnuts, and curds, and cream, shall be your fare;
The carpet-ground shall be with leaves o'erspread;
And boughs shall weave a covering for your head.
For, see, yon sunny hill the shade extends;
And curling smoke from cottages ascends.

Translated by John Dryden

Michael Drayton

From PASTORALLS, THE FOURTH EGLOGUE

When first religion with a golden chayne,
Men unto fayre civilitie did draw,
Who sent from heaven, brought justice forth againe,
To keepe the good, the viler sort to awe.

★　　★　　★

The tender grasse was then the softest bed:
The pleasant'st shades esteem'd the statelyest halls,
No belly-churle with Bacchus banqueted,
Nor painted rags then covered rotten walls:

★　　★　　★

But when the bowels of the earth were sought,
Whose golden entrailes mortalls did espie,
Into the world all mischiefe then was brought,
This fram'd the mint, that coyn'd our miserie.

The loftie pines were presently hew'd downe,
And men, sea-monsters swam the bracky flood,
In wainscote tubs to seeke out worlds unknowne,
For certayne ill, to leave assured good.

The steed was tamde and fitted to the field,
That serves a subject to the riders lawes,
He that before ranne in the pastures wyld,
Felt the stiffe curbe controule his angrie jawes.

The Cyclops then stood sweating to the fire,
The use thereof in softning metals found,
That did streight limbs in stubborne steele attire,
Forging sharpe tooles the tender flesh to wound.

The citie-builder, then intrencht his towres,
And laid his wealth within the walled towne,
Which afterward in rough and stormie stowres,
Kindled the fire that burnt his bulwarkes downe.

This was the sad beginning of our woe,
That was from hell on wretched mortals hurl'd,
And from this fount did all those mischiefes flow,
Whose inundation drowneth all the world.

Adrienne Rich

STUDY OF HISTORY

Out there.   The mind of the river
as it might be you.

Lights   blotted by unseen hulls
repetitive shapes passing
dull foam crusting the margin
barges sunk below the water-line with silence.
The scow, drudging on.

Lying in the dark, to think of you
and your harsh traffic
gulls pecking your rubbish   natural historians
mourning your lost purity
pleasure cruisers
witlessly careening you

but this
after all
is the narrows and after
all we have never entirely
known what was done to you upstream
what powers trepanned
which of your channels diverted
what rockface leaned to stare
in your upturned
defenseless
face.

Douris

EPHESOS

Clouds of the heavens,
   from where did you absorb
those disastrous floods
   which swamped everything
with unbroken night?
   These countless homes,
these properties of happy days belonged
   not to Libya, but
to Ephesos. Then where,
   where were its guardian spirits
looking? It was the most
   hymned of Ionian cities.
Along with the rolling waves
   everything ran out to sea,
with the flooding rivers.

Translated by Peter Jay

Elizabeth Weston

CONCERNING THE FLOODING OF PRAGUE AFTER CONSTANT RAINS

The unkind Skies have called up angry winds;
the troubled clouds are wet with constant rain.
The Molda, swelled by waves made savage by the storms
bursts through its ample sides, and pours great streams
over the spreading fields, then in its grasp
carries dry meadows away.
The foaming torrent gorges on all things,
the raging waters leave their mark of grief.
Here uprooted corn and fruits swept headlong by the flood,
there a man, a bed, a woman swirling past.
Look at the tree trunks, pine trees, see the roofs afloat,
portentous objects whirled on by the waves.
The deepened waters drown walled gardens now:
Thus all things perish underneath the seas!
A boat ploughs through the square, a fish defiles God's shrine;
runaway waters lap the altar steps.
Dazed crowds stand by, their garments streaming wet,
they grieve to see the wreck of all they own.
Such a sight it was to see the Molda rage;
so like the flood that Deucalion knew.
Oh Jove, who tames wild monsters of the deep,
incline your head and drown these many woes.

Translated by Susan Bassnett

George Awoonor-Williams

THE SEA EATS THE LAND AT HOME

At home the sea is in the town,
Running in and out of the cooking places,
Collecting the firewood from the hearths
And sending it back at night;
The sea eats the land at home.
It came one day at the dead of night,
Destroying the cement walls,
And carried away the fowls,
The cooking-pots and the ladles,
The sea eats the land at home;
It is a sad thing to hear the wails,
And the mourning shouts of the women,
Calling on all the gods they worship,
To protect them from the angry sea.
Aku stood outside where her cooking-pot stood,
With her two children shivering from the cold,
Her hands on her breast,
Weeping mournfully.
Her ancestors have neglected her,
Her gods have deserted her,
It was a cold Sunday morning,
The storm was raging,
Goats and fowls were struggling in the water,
The angry water of the cruel sea;
The lap-lapping of the bark water at the shore,
And above the sobs and the deep and low moans,
Was the eternal hum of the living sea.
It has taken away their belongings
Adena has lost the trinkets which
Were her dowry and her joy,
In the sea that eats the land at home,
Eats the whole land at home.

John Ceirog Hughes

THE MOUNTAIN STREAM

Mountain stream, clear and limpid, wandering down towards the valley, whispering songs among the rushes – oh, that I were as the stream!

Mountain heather all in flower – longing fills me, at the sight, to stay upon the hills in the wind and the heather.

Small birds of the high mountain that soar up in the healthy wind, flitting from one peak to the other – oh, that I were as the bird!

Son of the mountain am I, far from home making my song; but my heart is in the mountain, with the heather and small birds.

Anon [Eskimo]

'FAR INLAND'

Far inland
go my sad thoughts.
It is too much
never to leave this bench.
I want to wander
far inland.

I rememebr
hunting animals,
the good food.
It is too much
never to leave this bench.
I want to wander
far inland.

I hunted
like men. I carried
weapons, shot reindeer,
bull, cow, and calf,
killed them with my arrows
one evening
when almost winter
twilight fell
far inland.

I remember
how I struggled
inland
under the dropping sky
of snow.
The earth is white
far inland.

Translated by Willis Barnstone

W.S. Graham

LOCH THOM

1

Just for the sake of recovering
I walked backward from fifty-six
Quick years of age wanting to see,
And managed not to trip or stumble
To find Loch Thom and turned round
To see the stretch of my childhood
Before me. Here is the loch. The same
Long-beaked cry curls across
The heather-edges of the water held
Between the hills a boyhood's walk
Up from Greenock. It is the morning.

And I am here with my mammy's
Bramble jam scones in my pocket.
The Firth is miles and I have come
Back to find Loch Thom maybe
In this light does not recognise me.

This is a lonely freshwater loch.
No farms on the edge. Only
Heather grouse-moor stretching
Down to Greenock and One Hope
Street or stretching away across
Into the blue moors of Ayrshire.

2

And almost I am back again
Wading the heather down to the edge
To sit. The minnows go by in shoals
Like iron-filings in the shallows.

My mother is dead. My father is dead
And all the trout I used to know
Leaping from their sad rings are dead.

3

I drop my crumbs into the shallow
Weed for the minnows and pinheads.
You see that I will have to rise
And turn round and get back where
My running age will slow for a moment
To let me on. It is a colder
Stretch of water than I remember.

The curlew's cry travelling still
Kills me fairly. In front of me
The grouse flurry and settle. GOBACK
GOBACK GOBACK FAREWELL LOCH THOM.

Anger

'A perpetual/sour October'

Helen Dunmore

PLOUGHING THE ROUGHLANDS

It's not the four-wheeled drive crawler
spitting up dew and herbs,

not Dalapon followed by dressings
of dense phosphates,

nor ryegrass greening behind wire as behind glass,

not labourers wading in moonsuits
through mud gelded by paraquat –

but now, the sun-yellow, sky-blue
vehicles mount the pale chalk,

the sky bowls on the white hoops
and white breast of the roughland,

the farmer with Dutch eyes
guides forward the quick plough.

Now, flush after flush of Italian ryegrass
furs up the roughland

with its attentive, bright,
levelled-off growth –

pale monoculture
sweating off rivers of filth

fenced by the primary
colours of crawler and silo.

Wendell Berry

'I GO FROM THE WOODS'

I go from the woods into the cleared field:
A place no human made, a place unmade
By human greed, and to be made again.
Where centuries of leaves once built by dying
A deathless potency of light and stone
And mold of all that grew and fell, the timeless
Fell into time. The earth fled with the rain.
The growth of fifty thousand years undone
In a few careless seasons, stripped to rock
And clay – a 'new land', truly, that no race
Was ever native to, but hungry mice
And sparrows and the circling hawks, dry thorns
And thistles sent by generosity
Of new beginning. No Eden, this was
A garden once, a good and perfect gift;
Its possible abundance stood in it
As it then stood. But now what it might be
Must be foreseen, darkly, through many lives –
Thousands of years to make it what it was,
Beginning now, in our few troubled days.

Stevie Smith

ALONE IN THE WOODS

Alone in the woods I felt
The bitter hostility of the sky and the trees
Nature has taught her creatures to hate
Man that fusses and fumes
Unquiet man
As the sap rises in the trees
As the sap paints the trees a violent green
So rises the wrath of Nature's creatures
At man
So paints the face of Nature a violent green.
Nature is sick at man
Sick at his fuss and fume
Sick at his agonies
Sick at his gaudy mind
That drives his body
Ever more quickly
More and more
In the wrong direction.

Tom Murray

CUTTING A TRACK TO CARDWELL

The track is cleared
Trees have been cut down, for the highway
As a mother carries her child
So the horse bears its rider
To Cardwell, along a single track
We can see across the ocean to the mission
Having just come down the range

Along a single track to Cardwell
We can see across the ocean to the mission
Having just come down the range

A wide swath of trees
Cut to ground level
Trees in a wide swath
Cut to ground level
With steel axes
Cut so quickly
By a mob of men, chattering in English
Their voices echoing
English, spoken by a mob of men
Their voices echoing
As they work close together
Lips slapping as they talk
All talking at the same time

Translated from the Jirrbal dialect

Charlotte Mew

THE TREES ARE DOWN

– and he cried with a loud voice:
Hurt not the earth, neither the sea, nor the trees –
(Revelation)

They are cutting down the great plane-trees at the end of the garden.
    For days there has been the grate of the saw, the swish of the branches as they
        fall,
The crash of trunks, the rustle of trodden leaves,
With the 'Whoops' and the 'Whoas', the loud common talk, the loud common
    laughs of the men, above it all.

I remember one evening of a long past Spring
Turning in at a gate, getting out of a cart, and finding a large dead rat in the mud of
    the drive.
I remember thinking: alive or dead, a rat was a god-forsaken thing,
But at least, in May, that even a rat should be alive.
The week's work here is as good as done. There is just one bough
    On the roped bole, in the fine grey rain,
            Green and high
            And lonely against the sky.

(Down now!–)
   And but for that,
   If an old dead rat
Did once, for a moment, unmake the Spring, I might never have thought of him
  again.

It is not for a moment the Spring is unmade to-day;
These were great trees, it was in them from root to stem:
When the men with the 'Whoops' and the 'Whoas' have carted the whole of the
  whispering loveliness away
Half the Spring, for me, will have gone with them.

It is going now, and my heart has been struck with the hearts of the planes;
Half my life it has beat with these, in the sun, in the rains,
     In the March wind, the May breeze,
In the great gales that came over to them across the roofs from the great seas.
     There was only a quiet rain when they were dying;
     They must have heard the sparrows flying,
And the small creeping creatures in the earth where they were lying –
     But I, all day, I heard an angel crying:
        'Hurt not the trees'.

Elizabeth Carter

TO A GENTLEMAN, ON HIS INTENDING TO CUT DOWN A GROVE TO ENLARGE HIS PROSPECT

In plaintive sounds, that tun'd to woe
   The sadly-sighing breeze,
A weeping *Hamadryad* mourn'd
   Her fate-devoted trees.

Ah! Stop thy sacrilegious hand,
   Nor violate the shade,
Where nature form'd a silent haunt
   For contemplation's aid.

Canst thou, the son of science, bred
    Where learned Isis flows,
Forget that, nurs'd in shelt'ring groves,
    The *Grecian* genius rose?

Within the plantane's spreading shade
    Immortal *Plato* taught;
And fair *Lyceum* form'd the depth
    Of *Aristotle's* thought.

To *Latian* groves reflect thy views,
    And bless the *Tuscan* gloom;
Where eloquence deplor'd the fate
    Of Liberty and *Rome*.

Retir'd beneath the beechen shade,
    From each inspiring bough
The Muses wove th' unfading wreathes,
    That circled *Virgil's* brow.

Reflect, before the fatal ax
    My threaten'd doom has wrought;
Nor sacrifice to sensual taste
    The nobler growth of thought;

Not all the glowing fruits that blush,
    On *India's* sunny coast,
Can recompense thee for the worth
    Of one idea lost.

My shade a produce may supply
    Unknown to solar fire;
And what excludes *Apollo's* rage,
    Shall harmonize his lyre.

Norman Nicholson

THE ELM DECLINE

The crags crash to the tarn; slowmotion corrosion of scree.
From scooped corries,
bare as slag,
black sykes ooze
through quarries of broken boulders.
The sump of the tarn
slumps into its mosses — bog
asphodel, sundew, sedges —
a perpetual
sour October
yellowing the moor.

                    Seven
thousand years ago
trees grew
high as this tarn. The pikes
were stacks and skerries
spiking the green,
the tidal surge
of oak, birch, elm,
ebbing to ochre
and the wrackwood of backend.

                    Then
round the year Three
Thousand B.C.,
the proportion of elm pollen
preserved in peat
declined from twenty
per cent to four.

          Stone axes,
chipped clean from the crag-face,
ripped the hide off the fells.
Spade and plough
scriated the bared flesh,
skewered down to the bone.
The rake flaked into fragments
and kettlehole tarns
were shovelled chock-full
of a rubble of rotting rocks.

             Today

electric landslips
crack the rock;
drills tunnel it;
valleys go under the tap.
Dynamited runnels
channel a poisoned rain,
and the fractured ledges
are scoured and emery'd
by wind-to-wind rubbings
of nuclear dust.

           Soon
the pikes, the old
bottlestops of lava,
will stand scraped bare,
nothing but air round stone
and stone in air,
ground-down stumps
of a skeleton jaw —

           Until
under the scree
under the riddled rake,
beside the outflow of the reedless lake,
no human eye remains to see
a land-scape man
helped nature make.

Alexander Pope

From *AN ESSAY ON MAN*

EPISTLE I

Ask for what end the heav'nly bodies shine,
Earth for whose use? Pride answers, ''Tis for mine:
For me kind Nature wakes her genial pow'r,
Suckles each herb, and spreads out ev'ry flow'r;
Annual for me, the grape, the rose renew
The juice nectareous, and the balmy dew;
For me, the mine a thousand treasures brings;
For me, health gushes from a thousand springs;
Seas roll to waft me, suns to light me rise;
My foot-stool earth, my canopy the skies.

Andrew Marvell

THE MOWER AGAINST GARDENS

Luxurious man, to bring his vice in use,
    Did after him the world seduce,
And from the fields the flowers and plants allure,
    Where nature was most plain and pure.
He first enclosed within the gardens square
    A dead and standing pool of air,
And a more luscious earth for them did knead,
    Which stupefied them while it fed.
The pink grew then as double as his mind;
    The nutriment did change the kind.
With strange perfumes he did the roses taint,
    And flowers themselves were taught to paint.
The tulip, white, did for complexion seek,
    And learned to interline its cheek:
Its onion root they then so high did hold,
    That one was for a meadow sold.
Another world was searched, through oceans new,

To find the *Marvel of Peru*.
And yet these rarities might be allowed
   To man, that sovereign thing and proud,
Had he not dealt between the bark and tree,
   Forbidden mixtures there to see.
No plant now knew the stock from which it came;
   He grafts upon the wild the tame:
That th'uncertain and adulterate fruit
   Might put the palate in dispute.
His green seraglio has its eunuchs too,
   Lest any tyrant him outdo.
And in the cherry he does nature vex,
   To procreate without a sex.
'Tis all enforced, the fountain and the grot,
   While the sweet fields do lie forgot:
Where willing nature does to all dispense
   A wild and fragrant innocence:
And fauns and fairies do the meadows till,
   More by their presence than their skill.
Their statues, polished by some ancient hand,
   May to adorn the gardens stand:
But howsoe'er the figures do excel,
   The gods themselves with us do dwell.

Stevie Smith

'I LOVE THE ENGLISH COUNTRY SCENE'

I love the English country scene
But sometimes think there's too much Hooker's green,
Especially in August, when the flowers that might have lent a
Lightness, don't; being gamboge or magenta.

H. D.

SHELTERED GARDEN

I have had enough.
I gasp for breath.

Every way ends, every road,
every foot-path leads at last
to the hill-crest –
then you retrace your steps,
or find the same slope on the other side,
precipitate.

I have had enough –
border-pinks, clove-pinks, wax-lilies,
herbs, sweet-cress.

O for some sharp swish of a branch –
there is no scent of resin
in this place,
no taste of bark, of coarse weeds,
aromatic, astringent –
only border on border of scented pinks.

Have you seen fruit under cover
that wanted light –
pears wadded in cloth,
protected from the frost,
melons, almost ripe,
smothered in straw?

Why not let the pears cling
to the empty branch?
All your coaxing will only make
a bitter fruit –
let them cling, ripen of themselves,
test their own worth,
nipped, shrivelled by the frost,
to fall at last but fair
with a russet coat.

Or the melon –
let it bleach yellow
in the winter light,
even tart to the taste –
it is better to taste of frost –
the exquisite frost –
than of wadding and of dead grass.

For this beauty,
beauty without strength,
chokes out life.
I want wind to break,
scatter these pink-stalks,
snap off their spiced heads,
fling them about with dead leaves –
spread the paths with twigs,
limbs broken off,
trail great pine branches,
hurled from some far wood
right across the melon-patch,
break pear and quince –
leave half-trees, torn, twisted
but showing the fight was valiant.

O to blot out this garden
to forget, to find a new beauty
in some terrible
wind-tortured place.

Patrick Magill

From PADDING IT

You speak of the road in your verses, you picture the joy of it still,
You of the specs and the collars, you who are geese of the quill,
You pad it along with a wine-flask and your pockets crammed with
    dough,
Eat and drink at your pleasure, and write how the flowers grow –
If your stomach was empty as pity, your hobnails were down at the
    heels,
And a nor'easter biting your nose off, then you would know how it
    feels,
A nail in the shoe of your bluchers jagging your foot like a pin,
And every step on your journey was driving it further in,
Then, out on the great long roadway, you'd find when you went
    abroad,
The nearer you go to nature the further you go from God.

Charles Cotton

From THE WONDERS OF THE PEAKE

Durst I expostulate with *Providence*,
I then should ask, wherein the innocence
Of my poor undesigning infancy,
Could *Heaven* offend to such a black degree,
As for th'offence to damn me to a place
Where *Nature* only suffers in disgrace,
A *Country* so deform'd, the *Traveller*
Would swear those parts Natures *pudenda* were:
Like *Warts* and *Wens*, hills on the one side swell,
To all but *Natives* inaccessible;
Th'other a blue scrofulous scum defiles,
Flowing from th'earths impostumated boyles;
That seems the steps (Mountains on Mountains
    thrown)
By which the *Giants* storm'd the *Thunderers* throne,
This from that prospect seems the sulph'rous flood,
Where sinful *Sodom* and *Gomorrah* stood.

Maria Logan

VERSES ON HEARING THAT AN AIRY AND PLEASANT SITUATION, NEAR A POPULOUS AND COMMERCIAL TOWN, WAS SURROUNDED WITH NEW BUILDINGS

There was a time! that time the Muse bewails,
When Sunny Hill enjoyed refreshing gales;
When Flora sported in its fragrant bowers,
And strewed with liberal hand her sweetest flowers!
Now sable vapours pregnant with disease,
Clog the light pinions of the southern breeze;
Each verdant plant assumes a dusky hue,
And sooty atoms taint the morning dew.
No more the lily rears her spotless head,
Health, verdure, beauty, fragrance, all are fled:
Sulphureous clouds deform the rising day,
Nor own the power of Sol's meridian ray;
While sickly damps, from Aire's polluted stream,
Quench the pure radiance of his parting beam.
These are thy triumphs, Commerce! – these thy spoils!
Yet sordid mortals glory in their toils,
Spurn the pure joys which simple Nature yields,
Her breezy hills, dark groves, and verdant fields;
With cold indifference view her blooming charms,
And give youth, ease and health to thy enfeebling arms.

Ernesto Cardenal

NEW ECOLOGY

In September more coyotes were seen
            round San Ubaldo.
More alligators shortly after the triumph,
            in the rivers near San Ubaldo.
                More rabbits in the road and grisons . . .

The bird population has tripled, they say,
   especially the tree duck.
The noisy ducks fly down to swim
   where they see the water shining.

Somoza's men also destroyed
   lakes, rivers and mountains.
  They diverted rivers for their estates.
The Ochomogo dried up last summer.
The Sinecapa dried
  because of the great landowners' tree-felling.

The Matagalpa Rio Grande ran dry during the war,
   over the plains of Sebaco.
They built two dams on the Ochomogo
   and capitalist chemical waste
crashed into the river
   whose fish staggered like drunks.

   The River Boaco has filthy water
The Moyuá lagoon dried up. A Somoza colonel
stole the lands from the peasants and built a dam.
The Moyuá lagoon for centuries so lovely where it lay.
   (But now the little fishes will come back.)
   They felled and dammed.

   Few iguanas in the sun, few armadillos.
Somoza sold the green Caribbean turtle.
They exported sea turtle and iguana eggs in lorries.
   The caguama turtle is becoming extinct.

José Somoza has been putting an end
   to the sawfish in the Great Lake.
Extinction threatens the ocelot
   with its soft wood-coloured pelt,
and the puma and the tapir in the mountains
   (like the peasants in the mountains).

And poor River Chiquito! Its disgrace
shames the whole country.
              Somoza's ways befouling its waters.
The River Chiquito of León, choked with sewage,
and effluent from soap and tanning factories,
white waste from soap, red from tanneries,
its bed bestrewn with plastic junk,
                    chamber pots and rusty iron.
That was Somoza's legacy.
(We must see it running clear and sweet again
             singing its way to the sea.)

All Managua's filthy water in Lake Managua
and chemical waste
          And over in Solentiname
on the isle of La Zanata a bg white heap
           of stinking sawfish bones.

But now the sawfish and the freshwater shark
can breathe again.
Once more Tisma's waters mirror many herons.
It has lots of little grackles,
         garganeys, tree ducks, kiskadees.

   And flowers are flourishing.
Armadillos are very happy with this government.
   We are recovering forests, streams, lagoons.
We are going to decontaminate Lake Managua.

Not only humans longed for liberation.
All ecology groaned. The revolution
is also for animals, rivers, lakes and trees.

              Translated by Dinah Livingstone

Anna Seward

From COLEBROOK DALE

Scene of superfluous grace and wasted bloom,
O, violated Colebrook! in an hour,
To beauty unpropitious and to song,
The Genius of thy shades, by Plutus brib'd,
Amid thy grassy lanes, thy woodwild glens,
Thy knolls and bubbling wells, thy rocks, and streams,
Slumbers! – while tribes fuliginous invade
The soft, romantic, consecrated scenes;
Haunt of the wood-nymph, who with airy step,
In times long vanish'd, through thy pathless groves
Rang'd; – while the pearly-wristed Naiads lean'd,
Braiding their light locks o'er thy crystal flood,
Shadowy and smooth. What, though to vulgar eye
Invisible, yet oft the lucid gaze
Of the rapt Bard, in every dell and glade
Beheld them wander; – saw, from the clear wave
Emerging, all the watry sisters rise,
Weaving the aqueous lily, and the flag,
In wreaths fantastic, for the tresses bright
Of amber-hair'd Sabrina. – Now we view
Their fresh, their fragrant, and their silent reign
Usurpt by Cyclops; – hear, in mingled tones,
Shout their throng'd barge, their pond'rous engines
      clang
Through thy coy dales: while red the countless fires,
With umber'd flames, bicker on all thy hills
Dark'ning the Summer's sun with columns large
Of thick, sulphureous smoke, which spread, like palls,
That screen the dead, upon the sylvan robe
Of thy aspiring rocks; pollute thy gales,
And stain thy glassy waters. – See, in troops,
The dusk artificers, with brazen throats,
Swarm on thy cliffs, and clamour in thy glens,
Steepy and wild, ill suited to such guests.

★　　★　　★

Warn'd by the Muse, if Birmingham should draw,
In future years, from more congenial climes
Her massy ore, her labouring sons recall,
And sylvan Colebrook's winding vales restore
To beauty and to song, content to draw
From unpoetic scenes her rattling stores,
Massy and dun; if, thence supplied, she fail,
Britain, to glut thy rage commercial, see
Grim Wolverhampton lights her smouldering fires,
And Sheffield, smoke-involv'd; dim where she
      stands
Circled by lofty mountains, which condense
Her dark and spiral wreaths to drizzling rains,
Frequent and sullied; as the neighbouring hills
Ope their deep veins and feed her cavern'd flames;
While, to her dusky sister, Ketley yields,
From her long-desolate, and livid breast,
The ponderous metal. No aerial forms
On Sheffield's arid moor, or Ketley's heath,
E'er wove the floral crowns, or smiling stretch'd
The shelly scepter; – there no Poet rov'd
To catch bright inspirations. Blush, ah, blush,
Thou venal Genius of these outraged groves,
And thy apostate head with thy soil'd wings
Veil! – who hast thus thy beauteous charge resign'd
To habitants ill-suited; hast allow'd
Their rattling forges, and their hammer's din,
And hoarse, rude throats, to fright the gentle train,
Dryads, and fair hair'd Naiades: – the song,
Once loud as sweet, of the wild woodland choir
To silence; – disenchant the poet's spell,
And to a gloomy Erebus transform
The destined rival of Tempean vales.

Marion Bernstein

A SONG OF GLASGOW TOWN

I'll sing a song of Glasgow town,
That stands on either side
The river that was once so fair,
The much insulted Clyde.
That stream, once pure, but now so foul,
Was never made to be
A sewer, just to bear away
The refuse to the sea.
Oh, when will Glasgow's factories
Cease to pollute its tide,
And let the Glasgow people see
The beauty of the Clyde!

I'll sing a song of Glasgow town:
On every side I see
A crowd of giant chimney stalks
As grim as grim can be.
There's always smoke from some of them –
Some black, some brown, some grey
Yet genius has invented means
To burn the smoke away.
Oh, when will Glasgow factories
Cease to pollute the air;
To spread dull clouds o'er sunny skies
That should be bright and fair!

I'll sing a song of Glasgow town,
Where wealth and want abound;
Where the high seat of learning dwells
Mid ignorance profound.
Oh, when will Glasgow make a rule
To do just what she ought –
Let starving bairns in every school
Be fed as well as taught!
And when will Glasgow city be
Fair Caledonia's pride,
And boast her clear unclouded skies,
And crystal-flowing Clyde?

Juvenal

From SATIRE III

Who fears in country towns a house's fall,
Or to be caught betwixt a riven wall?
But we inhabit a weak city here;
Which buttresses and props but scarcely bear:
And 'tis the village mason's daily calling,
To keep the world's metropolis from falling,
To cleanse the gutters, and the chinks to close;
And, for one night, secure his lord's repose.
At Cumae we can sleep quite round the year,
Nor falls, nor fires, nor nightly dangers fear;
While rolling flames from Roman turrets fly,
And the pale citizens for buckets cry.
Thy neighbour has removed his wretched store
(Few hands will rid the lumber of the poor);
Thy own third story smokes, while thou, supine,
Art drench'd in fumes of undigested wine.
For if the lowest floors already burn,
Cocklofts and garrets soon will take the turn;
Where thy tame pigeons next the tiles were bred,
Which, in their nests unsafe, are timely fled.

★   ★   ★

'Tis frequent here for want of sleep, to die;
Which fumes of undigested feasts deny;
And, with imperfect heat, in languid stomachs fry.
What house secure from noise the poor can keep,
When e'en the rich can scarce afford to sleep:
So dear it costs to purchase rest in Rome;
And hence the sources of diseases come.
The drover who his fellow drover meets
In narrow passages of winding streets;
The wagoners that curse their standing teams,
Would wake e'en drowsy Drusius from his dreams.

      ★   ★   ★

Return we to the dangers of the night:
And first behold our houses' dreadful height;
From whence come broken potsherds tumbling
    down;
And leaky ware from garret windows thrown:
Well may they break our heads, that mark the
    flinty stone:
'Tis want of sense to sup abroad too late;
Unless thou first hast settled thy estate.
As many fates attend thy steps to meet
As there are waking windows in the street.
Bless the good gods, and think thy chance is rare
To have a pisspot only for thy share.

Translated by John Dryden

Margaret Walker

SORROW HOME

My roots are deep in southern life; deeper than John Brown
    or Nat Turner or Robert Lee. I was sired and weaned
    in a tropic world. The palm tree and banana leaf,
    mango and coconut, breadfruit and rubber trees know
    me.

Warm skies and gulf blue streams are in my blood. I belong
with the smell of fresh pine, with the trail of coon, and
the spring growth of wild onion.

I am no hothouse bulb to be reared in steam heated flats
with the music of El and subway in my ears, walled in
by steel and wood and brick far from the sky.

I want the cotton fields, tobacco and the cane. I want to
walk along with sacks of seed to drop in fallow ground.
Restless music is in my heart and I am eager to be
gone.

O Southland, sorrow home, melody beating in my bone and
blood! How long will the Klan of hate, the hounds and
the chain gangs keep me from my own?

Thadious M. Davis

'HONEYSUCKLE WAS THE SADDEST ODOR OF ALL, I THINK'

Quentin Compson in Faulkner's
The Sound and the Fury

I wanted to be a nature poet
And write hauntingly of
Southern landscapes
Lush with brilliant birds
Animals green framed in hanging moss
Musky magnolia floral curtains
Under spiraling
Hot blue white moon spaces
Faulkner's wisteria
Lemon scented verbena
Sculptured yards luminous on
Twilight canvas blending
Cable's bayou parish
In painted midnight readings

I forgot 'Poplar trees bear a
Strange Fruit'
Deep roots
Strong limbs
Flexing
Spreading
North
Searing cultured descendants of
Fiery abolitionists

In frigid light
School buses plow
Push thunder through
Brick-lined rotaries
Spinning salt-snow
Pebble bouquets
In frozen dark
Spit slices my pores
Hard glass fragments
Jagged tears
Remnants of
My poetic eye

R.S. Thomas

AUTUMN ON THE LAND

A man, a field, silence – what is there to say?
He lives, he moves, and the October day
Burns slowly down
                History is made
Elsewhere; the hours forfeit to time's blade
Don't matter here. The leaves large and small,
Shed by the branches, unlamented fall
About his shoulders. You may look in vain
Through the eyes' window; on his meagre hearth
The thin, shy soul has not begun its reign
Over the darkness. Beauty, love and mirth
And joy are strangers there.
                    You must revise
Your bland philosophy of nature, earth
Has of itself no power to make men wise.

Sylvia Plath

GREEN ROCK, WINTHROP BAY

No lame excuses can gloss over
Barge-tar clotted at the tide-line, the wrecked pier.
I should have known better.

Fifteen years between me and the bay
Profited memory, but did away with the old scenery
And patched this shoddy

Makeshift of a view to quit
My promise of an idyll, the blue's worn out:
It's a niggard estate,

Inimical now. The great green rock
We gave good use as ship and house is black
With tarry muck

And periwinkles, shrunk to common
Size. The cries of scavenging gulls sound thin
In the traffic of planes

From Logan Airport opposite.
Gulls circle gray under shadow of a steelier flight.
Loss cancels profit.

Unless you do this tawdry harbor
A service and ignore it, I go a liar
Gilding what's eyesore,

Or must take loophole and blame time
For the rock's dwarfed lump, for the drabbled scum,
For a churlish welcome.

Sheenagh Pugh

AFTER I CAME BACK FROM ICELAND

After I came back from Iceland,
I couldn't stop talking. It was the light,
you see, the light and the air. I tried to put it
into poems, even, but you couldn't write

the waterfall on White River, blinding
and glacial, nor the clean toy town
with the resplendent harbour for its glass.
You couldn't write how the black lava shone,

nor how the outlines of the bright red roofs
cut the sky sharp as a knife; how breathing
was like drinking cold water. When I got back
to Heathrow and walked out into Reading,

I damn near choked on this warm gritty stuff
I called air; also on the conjecture
that we'd all settle for second best
once we'd forgotten there was something more.

Terri Meyette

CELEBRATION 1982

They say no one died.
Tiny desert flower
micro beetle bug
are they not life?
Their bag of bones
blown into the wind
captured in white dust storms
washed down polluted rivers
are they not dead?

They say no one died.
Scientist, unconscious
mushroom button pushers,
Secretary of Defense what's his name,
President what's his name
when will they be tried
for imposing fantasies and celebrations
on all life forms?

It wasn't enough
in '45'
Hiroshima and Nagasaki.

They say no one died.
Nevada desert
1000 miles into her bowels
earth melted.

radiation, radiation, radiation,
radiation.
oozed into blood
of Shoshone and Paiute.
The bomb lasted minutes
the intent lasts generations
in the womb of Creation, herself.

They say no one died.
Closing their eye,
they dismissed death
dismissed life
became blinded
by white flash
their God.

They say no one died.
As thousands of beetles
fell through the sky
and rabbit hair turned into
fur coats protecting atoms
as they floated into water.
They won't look
they will just say
no one died.

Martyn Crucefix

MIKHAEL AT VIKSJÖN

They stopped bombing the lake with lime
a year ago. The helicopters stopped coming.
To see where it's unnaturally dark;
daylight vanishes undiminished to the bed.
I think of it as an absence of energy –
accepting everything and like the old
giving nothing back.

I hate them for it. The grey men who say
it's the British unfurling filthy flags,
blurting a language so strong it burns trees,
blackens the water, scalds memory clean
for a better world. Well, I've seen it:
I dreamed a sun above a dry, scuffed land
bleached white but for two mud-dark shelters,
lean-tos like wedges laid flat to the ground.
That was all. I tore every useless permit
I had, threw the scraps to the lake
wanting to see them shrivel into flame
as they touched the water.

I used to swim from the speckled rocks.
Swallows flashed above like fish through a lake.
First signs came with bright weather.
The water a lacklustre eye squeezed
under a skyline of pine like quills.
At the beach, the white bellies of perfect bream.

Then the helicopters waited till dusk
to drop their white loads crashing
and fizzing on the lake,
scrawling its surface like a mist.
Now they've stopped bombing and I no longer
think I see the tell-tale rings of rising fish.
Their splash would always hush the lake.
Now there is only a more difficult quiet,
one I use only for the anger which will not
follow the daylight to the bottom
but which comes clattering back at me off
the blackened water, louder and clearer,
louder and clearer!

Consolation

'Moments of an azure hue'

John Clare

COME HITHER

Come hither, ye who thirst;
Pure still the brook flows on;
Its waters are not curst;
Clear from its rock of stone
It bubbles and it boils,
An everlasting rill,
Then eddies and recoils
And wimples clearer still.
Art troubled? then come hither,
And taste of peace for ever.

Art weary? here's the place
For weariness to rest,
These flowers are herbs of grace
To cure the aching breast;
Soft beds these mossy banks
Where dewdrops only weep,
Where Nature 'turns God thanks
And sings herself to sleep.
Art troubled with strife? come hither,
Here's peace and summer weather.

Come hither for pleasure who list –
Here are oak boughs for a shade:
These leaves they will hide from the mist
Ere the sun his broad disk has displayed.
Here is peace if thy bosom be troubled,
Here is rest – if thou'rt weary, sit down –
Here pleasure you'll find it is doubled,
For content is life's only crown.
Disciples of sorrow, come hither,
For no blasts my joys can wither.

Art sick of the naughty world?
There's many been sick before thee;
Then leave these young shoots with their tendrils curled
For the oaks that are mossy and hoary.
Art weary with beating the flood
Here's a mossy bank – come and sit down:
'Twas Nature that planted this wood,
Unknown to the sins of the town
Full of pride and contention – come hither,
We'll talk of our troubles together.

The world is all lost in commotion,
The blind lead the blind into strife;
Come hither, thou wreck of life's ocean,
Let solitude warm thee to life.
Be the pilgrim of love and the joy of its sorrow,
Be anything but the world's man:
The dark of to-day brings the sun of to-morrow,
Be proud that your joy here began.
Poor shipwreck of life, journey hither,
And we'll talk of life's troubles together.

Claude McKay

AFTER THE WINTER

Some day, when trees have shed their leaves
    And against the morning's white
The shivering birds beneath the eaves
    Have sheltered for the night,
We'll turn our faces southward, love,
    Toward the summer isle
Where bamboos spire the shafted grove
    And wide-mouthed orchids smile.

And we will seek the quiet hill
   Where towers the cotton tree,
And leaps the laughing crystal rill,
   And works the droning bee.
And we will build a cottage there
   Beside an open glade,
With black-ribbed bluebells blowing near,
   And ferns that never fade.

William Butler Yeats

THE LAKE ISLE OF INNISFREE

I will arise and go now, and go to Innisfree,
And a small cabin build there, of clay and wattles made:
Nine bean-rows will I have there, a hive for the honey-
   bee,
And live alone in the bee-loud glade.

And I shall have some peace there, for peace comes
   dropping slow,
Dropping from the veils of the morning to where the
   cricket sings;
There midnight's all a glimmer, and noon a purple
   glow,
And evening full of the linnet's wings.

I will arise and go now, for always night and day
I hear lake water lapping with low sounds by the shore;
While I stand on the roadway, or on the pavements
   grey,
I hear it in the deep heart's core.

Charlotte Brontë

SPEAK OF THE NORTH

Speak of the North! A lonely moor
Silent and dark and trackless swells,
The waves of some wild streamlet pour
Hurriedly through its ferny dells.

Profoundly still the twilight air,
Lifeless the landscape; so we deem
Till like a phantom gliding near
A stag bends down to drink the stream.

And far away a mountain zone,
A cold, white waste of snow-drifts lies,
And one star, large and soft and lone,
Silently lights the unclouded skies.

Frances Bellerby

PLASH MILL, UNDER THE MOOR

The wind leapt, mad-wolf, over the rim of the moor
At a single bound, and with furious uproar
Fell on the tree-ringed house by the deep-cut stream –
Quiet little house standing alone,
Blind, old, pale as the moon,
And sunk in some ancient grassy dream.

Through all the roaring maniac din
Outside, the shadowless stillness there within
Held. No face, all the frantic day,
Pressed the glass, watching the green apple hailstorm,
No child's heart gladdened at thought of where acorns lay,
And beechnuts, treasure for harvesting safe from harm.

Now, firewood in the ragged grass will waste, sodden
Under the winter trees; and the darkening apples lie hidden;
And the driven leaves at the door stay huddled in vain,
Or, death-brittle, float on the floor under the broken pane.
But when, next March perhaps, sunlight the colour of frost
Wavers through branches to honeycomb some flaking wall
Changeless since autumn that will be the utmost
Hope realised: light's delicate miracle
Of grace
Still wrought on the forsaken place.

Rainer Maria Rilke

EARLY SPRING

Harshness gone. And sudden mitigation
laid upon the field's uncovered grey.
Little runnels change their intonation.
Tentative caresses stray

round the still earth from immensity.
Roads run far into the land, foretelling.
Unexpectedly you find it, welling
upwards in the empty tree.

Translated by J. B. Leishman

Anna Akhmatova

TASHKENT BREAKS INTO BLOSSOM

1

As if somebody ordered it
the city suddenly became bright –
every courtyard was visited
by white, light apparitions.
Their breathing is more understandable than words,
but their likeness is doomed to lie
at the bottom of the ditch
under the burning blue sky.

2

I will remember the roof of stars
and the radiance of eternal glory,
and the little kids
in the young arms
of dark-haired mothers.

Translated by Richard McKane

Anna Akhmatova

'EVERYTHING IS PLUNDERED . . .'

Everything is plundered, betrayed, sold,
Death's great black wing scrapes the air,
Misery gnaws to the bone.
Why then do we not despair?

By day, from the surrounding woods,
cherries blow summer into town;
at night the deep transparent skies
glitter with new galaxies.

And the miraculous comes so close
to the ruined, dirty houses –
something not known to anyone at all,
but wild in our breast for centuries.

Mieczyslaw Jastrun

BEYOND TIME

I am not concerned at all with the golden age of those
    pines
Or the white time of a carnation
Or the time of the dust on the highway
Or the time of passing clouds.
Whether I lived an age or an instant loses its importance.
It is enough to glance into the eyes of a sunflower,
To grind up thyme in your hand,
Any scent in the infinitive suffices,
Any of the usually unnoticed things of the earth,
Suddenly perceived in such a way
That their shape with eyelids not quite closed
Denies transience (of water, of clouds, of man).

Translated by Czeslaw Milosz

Anon [Eskimo]

DELIGHT IN NATURE

Isn't it delightful,
little river cutting through the gorge,
when you slowly approach it,
and trout hang behind stones
in the stream?
    Jajai–ija.

Isn't it delightful,
that *grassy* river bank?
Yet Willow Twig.
whom I so long to see again,
is lost to me.
So be it.
The winding of the river
through the gorge is lovely enough.
    Jajai–ija.

Isn't it delightful
that bluish island of rocks out there,
as you slowly approach it?
So what does it matter
that the blowing spirit of the air
wanders over the rocks:
the island is so beautiful,
when, driving steadily,
you gain on it.

Translated by Tom Lowenstein

John Keats

ON THE GRASSHOPPER AND CRICKET

The poetry of earth is never dead:
   When all the birds are faint with the hot sun,
   And hide in cooling trees, a voice will run
From hedge to hedge about the new-mown mead –
That is the Grasshopper's. He takes the lead
   In summer luxury; he has never done
   With his delights, for when tired out with fun
He rests at ease beneath some pleasant weed.
The poetry of earth is ceasing never:
   On a lone winter evening when the frost
      Has wrought a silence, from the stove there shrills
The Cricket's song, in warmth increasing ever,
   And seems to one in drowsiness half lost,
      The Grasshopper's among some grassy hills.

Byron

From CHILDE HAROLD'S PILGRIMAGE

THE OCEAN

There is a pleasure in the pathless woods,
There is a rapture on the lonely shore,
There is society, where none intrudes,
By the deep Sea, and music in its roar:
I love not Man the less, but Nature more,
From these our interviews, in which I steal
From all I may be, or have been before,
To mingle with the Universe, and feel
What I can ne'er express, yet can not all conceal.

Roll on, thou deep and dark blue Ocean – roll!
Ten thousand fleets sweep over thee in vain;
Man marks the earth with ruin – his control
Stops with the shore; upon the watery plain
The wrecks are all thy deed, nor doth remain
A shadow of man's ravage, save his own,
When, for a moment, like a drop of rain,
He sinks into thy depths with bubbling groan,
Without a grave, unknell'd, uncoffin'd and unknown.

His steps are not upon thy paths, – thy fields
Are not a spoil for him, – thou dost arise
And shake him from thee; the vile strength he wields
For earth's destruction thou dost all despise,
Spurning him from thy bosom to the skies,
And send'st him, shivering in thy playful spray
And howling to his Gods, where haply lies
His petty hope in some near port or bay,
And dashest him again to earth: – there let him lay.

The armaments which thunderstrike the walls
Of rock-built cities, bidding nations quake,
And monarchs tremble in their capitals,
The oak leviathans, whose huge ribs make
Their clay creator the vain title take
Of Lord of thee, and arbiter of war –
These are thy toys, and, as the snowy flake,
They melt into thy yeast of waves, which mar
Alike the Armada's pride or spoils of Trafalgar.

Thy shores are empires, changed in all save thee –
Assyria, Greece, Rome, Carthage, what are they?
Thy waters wash'd them power while they were free,
And many a tyrant since; their shores obey
The stranger, slave, or savage; their decay
Has dried up realms to deserts: – not so thou:–
Unchangeable, save to thy wild waves' play,
Time writes no wrinkle on thine azure brow:
Such as creation's dawn beheld, thou rollest now.

Thou glorious mirror, where the Almighty's form
Glasses itself in tempests; in all time, –
Calm or convulsed, in breeze, or gale, or storm,
Icing the pole, or in the torrid clime
Dark-heaving – boundless, endless, and sublime,
The image of eternity, the throne
Of the Invisible; even from out thy slime
The monsters of the deep are made; each zone
Obeys thee; thou goest forth, dread, fathomless, alone.

And I have loved thee, Ocean! and my joy
Of youthful sports was on thy breast to be
Borne, like thy bubbles, onward: from a boy
I wanton'd with thy breakers – they to me
Were a delight; and if the freshening sea
Made them a terror – 'twas a pleasing fear,
For I was as it were a child of thee,
And trusted to thy billows far and near,
And laid my hand upon thy mane – as I do here.

Kathleen Raine

HEIRLOOM

She gave me childhood's flowers,
Heather and wild thyme,
Eyebright and tormentil,
Lichen's mealy cup
Dry on wind-scored stone,
The corbies on the rock,
The rowan by the burn.

Sea-marvels a child beheld
Out in the fisherman's boat,
Fringed pulsing violet
Medusa, sea-gooseberries,
Starfish on the sea-floor,
Cowries and rainbow-shells
From pools on a rocky shore.

Gave me her memories,
But kept her last treasure:
'When I was a lass,' she said,
'Sitting among the heather,
'Suddenly I saw
'That all the moor was alive!
'I have told no one before'.

That was my mother's tale.
Seventy years had gone
Since she saw the living skein
Of which the world is woven,
And having seen, knew all;
Through long indifferent years
Treasuring the priceless pearl.

Paula Gunn Allen

KOPIS'TAYA
(*A Gathering of Spirits*)

Because we live in the browning season
the heavy air blocking our breath,
and in this time when living
is only survival, we doubt the voices
that come shadowed on the air,
that weave within our brains
certain thoughts, a motion that is soft,
imperceptible, a twilight rain
soft feather's fall, a small body
dropping into its nest, rustling, murmuring,
settling in for the night.

Because we live in the hardedged season,
where plastic brittle and gleaming shines
and in this space that is cornered and angled,
we do not notice wet, moist, the significant
drops falling in perfect spheres
that are the certain measures of our minds;
almost invisible, those tears,
soft as dew, fragile, that cling to leaves,
petals, roots, gentle and sure,
every morning.

We are the women of daylight; of clocks and steel
foundrys, of drugstores, and streetlights,
of superhighways that slice our days in two.
Wrapped around in glass and steel we ride
our lives; behind dark glasses we hide our eyes,
our thoughts, shaded, seem obscure, smoke
fills our minds, whisky husks our songs,
polyester cuts our bodies from our breath,
our feet from the welcoming stones of earth.
Our dreams are pale memories of themselves,
and nagging doubt is the false measure of our day.

Even so, the spirit voices are singing,
their thoughts are dancing in the dirty air.
Their feet touch the cement, the asphalt
delighting, still they weave dreams upon our
shadowed skulls, if we could listen.
If we could hear.
Let's go then. Let's find them. Let's
listen for the water, the careful gleaming drops
that glisten on the leaves, the flowers. Let's
ride the midnight, the early dawn. Feel the wind
striding through our hair. Let's dance
the dance of feathers, the dance of birds.

Joyce Isabel Lee

GRANITE CALL

Flat footed plains child
I'm lifted
through sunlit air
to the Grampians,
a million miles of sky,
blue forged and folded into rock.

On picnics
walking its wonderland,
granite holds me,
brown-faced scarps burn
bushfire-red at sunset.
All the colours more than earth.

Away on Cornwall's
granite cliffs, I step into
my grandfather's
secure young feet.
Over alien undercurrents
his call finds me.

Home in suburbia's
blocked brick, smooth
paved streets, through cloud,
Cornwall to the Grampians
rock to rock
I hear the call of granite.

Charles Tomlinson

THE MARL PITS

It was a language of water, light and air
   I sought – to speak myself free of a world
Whose stoic lethargy seemed the one reply
   To horizons and to streets that blocked them back
In a monotone fume, a bloom of grey.
   I found my speech. The years return me
To tell of all that seasoned and imprisoned:
   I breathe familiar, sedimented air
From a landscape of disembowellings, underworlds
   Unearthed among the clay. Digging
The marl, they dug a second nature
   And water, seeping up to fill their pits,
Sheeted them to lakes that wink and shine
   Between tips and steeples, streets and waste
In slow reclaimings, shimmers, balancings,
   As if kindling Eden rescinded its own loss
And words and water came of the same source.

Yüan Chieh

STONE FISH LAKE

I loved you dearly, Stone Fish Lake,
With your rock-island shaped like a swimming fish!
On the fish's back is the Wine-cup Hollow
And round the fish – the flowing waters of the Lake.
The boys on the shore sent little wooden ships,
Each made to carry a single cup of wine.
The island-drinkers emptied the liquor boats
And set their sails and sent them back for more.
On the shores of the Lake were jutting slabs of rock
And under the rocks there flowed an icy stream.
Heated with wine, to rinse our mouths and hands
In those cold waters was a joy beyond compare!

Of gold and jewels I have not any need;
For Caps and Coaches I do not care at all.
But I wish I could sit on the rocky banks of the Lake
For ever and ever staring at the Stone Fish.

Translated by Arthur Waley

William Barnes

TREES BE COMPANY

When zummer's burnen het's a-shed
Upon the droopen grasses head,
A-drevèn under sheädy leaves
The workvo'k in their snow-white sleeves,
We then mid yearn to clim' the height,
    Where thorns be white, above the vern;
An' aïr do turn the zunsheen's might
    To softer light too weak to burn –
        On woodless downs we mid be free,
        But lowland trees be company.

Though downs mid show a wider view
O' green a-reachen into blue
Than roads a-winden in the glen,
An' ringen wi' the sounds o' men;
The thissle's crown o' red an' blue.
    In Fall's cwold dew do wither brown,
An' larks come down 'ithin the lew,
    As storms do brew, an' skies do frown –
        An' though the down do let us free,
        The lowland trees be company.

Where birds do zing, below the zun,
In trees above the blue-smok'd tun,
An' sheädes o' stems do overstratch
The mossy path 'ithin the hatch;
If leaves be bright up over head,
   When Maÿ do shed its glitt'ren light;
Or, in the blight o' Fall, do spread
   A yollow bed avore our zight –
     Whatever season it mid be,
     The trees be always company.

When dusky night do nearly hide
The path along the hedge's zide,
An' daylight's hwomely sounds be still
But sounds o' water at the mill;
Then if noo feäce we long'd to greet
   Could come to meet our lwonesome treäce;
Or if noo peäce o' weary veet,
   However fleet, could reach its pleäce –
     However lwonesome we mid be,
     The trees would still be company.

William Drummond

'THRISE HAPPIE HEE, WHO BY SOME SHADIE GROVE'

Thrise happie hee, who by some shadie Grove
Farre from the clamorous World doth live his owne,
Though solitarie, yet who is not alone,
But doth converse with that *Eternall Love*.
O how more sweet is Birds harmonious Mone,
Or the soft Sobbings of the widow'd Dove?
Than those smoothe Whisp'rings neare a Princes Throne,
Which Good make doubtfull, doe the Evill approve.
O how more sweet is *Zephyres* wholesome Breath,
And Sighs perfum'd, which doe the Flowres unfold,
Than that Applause vaine *Honour* doth bequeath?
How sweete are Streames to Poyson drunke in Gold?
    The World is full of Horrours, Falshoods, Slights,
    Woods silent Shades have only true Delights.

John Milton

From PARADISE LOST
BOOK IV

Now nearer, crowns with her enclosure green,
As with a rural mound, the champaign head
Of a steep wilderness, whose hairy sides
With thicket overgrown, grotesque and wild,
Access denied; and overhead upgrew
Insuperable height of loftiest shade,
Cedar, and pine, and fir, and branching palm,
A sylvan scene, and, as the ranks ascend
Shade above shade, a woody theatre
Of stateliest view. Yet higher than their tops
The verdurous wall of Paradise upsprung,
Which to our general sire gave prospect large
Into his nether empire neighbouring round.
And higher than that wall a circling row
Of goodliest trees, loaden with fairest fruit,
Blossoms and fruits at once of golden hue,

Appeared, with gay enamelled colours mixed,
On which the sun more glad impressed his beams
Than in fair evening cloud, or humid bow,
When God hath showered the earth: so lovely seemed
That landscape; and of pure, now purer air
Meets his approach, and to the heart inspires
Vernal delight and joy, able to drive
All sadness but despair.

Mary Leapor

A SUMMER'S WISH

My guardian, bear me on thy downy wing
To some cool shade where infant flowers spring;
Where on the trees sweet honey-suckles blow,
And ruddy daisies paint the ground below:
Where the shrill linnet charms the solemn shade,
And zephyrs pant along the cooler glade,
Or shake the bull-rush by a river side,
While the gay sun-beams sparkle on the tide:
O for some grot whose rustick sides declare,
Ease, and not splendor, was the builder's care;
Where roses spread their unaffected charms,
And the curl'd vine extends her clasping arms;
Where happy silence lulls the quiet soul,
And makes it calm as summer waters roll.
Here let me learn to check each growing ill,
And bring to reason disobedient will;
To watch this incoherent breast, and find
What fav'rite passions rule the giddy mind.

Here no reproaches grate the wounded ear;
We see delighted, and transported hear:
While the glad warblers wanton round the trees,
And the still waters catch the dying breeze,
Grief waits without, and melancholy gloom:
Come, cheerful hope, and fill the vacant room;
Come ev'ry thought, which virtue gave to please;
Come, smiling health! with thy companion ease:
Let these, and all that virtue's self attends,
Bless the still hours of my gentle friends:
Peace to my foes, if any such there be,
And gracious heav'n give repose to me.

Lenrie Peters

AUTUMN BURNS ME

Autumn burns me with
primaeval fire. Makes my skin
taut with expectation,
hurls me out of summer fatigue
on to a new Bridge of Sighs.

Somewhere I feel the heart
of the earth pumping, and down below
it bleeds in a million ripples.
I drop a sweet memory into
the flow and the cascading grips me with fascination

Great trees in transit fall
are made naked in languor of shame
solitary like actors on a stage
like stars, orphans, celebrities,
politicians, uncomfortably mysteriously like you and me.

But I will not mourn the sadness.
I will go dead-leaf gathering
for the fire in a slice of sunlight
to fill my lungs with odours of decay
and my eyes with mellowed rainbow colours

I will go creeping down tasselled
latticed tree-avenues of light
and listen to squirrel tantrums
punctuate the orchestration of autumn silence
and hold in my hand the coiling stuff of nature

Then I will love
Yes love; extravagantly under
the flutter of dying leaves
and in a shadow of mist
in wonder; for autumn is wonder and wonder is hope.

Henry Thoreau

WITHIN THE CIRCUIT OF THIS PLODDING LIFE

Within the circuit of this plodding life
There enter moments of an azure hue,
Untarnished fair as is the violet
Or anemone, when the spring strews them
By some meandering rivulet, which make
The best philosophy untrue that aims
But to console man for his grievances.
I have remembered when the winter came,
High in my chamber in the frosty nights,
When in the still light of the cheerful moon,
On every twig and rail and jutting spout,
The icy spears were adding to their length
Against the arrows of the coming sun,
How in the shimmering noon of summer past
Some unrecorded beam slanted across
The upland pastures where the Johnswort grew;
Or heard, amid the verdure of my mind,

The bee's long smothered hum, on the blue flag
Loitering amidst the mead; or busy rill,
Which now through all its course stands still and dumb
Its own memorial, – purling at its play
Along the slopes, and through the meadows next,
Until its youthful sound was hushed at last
In the staid current of the lowland stream;
Or seen the furrows shine but late upturned,
And where the fieldfare followed in the rear,
When all the fields around lay bound and hoar
Beneath a thick integument of snow.
So by God's cheap economy made rich
To go upon my winter's task again.

Ivor Gurney

THE SOAKING

The rain has come, and the earth must be very glad
Of its moisture, and the made roads all dust clad;
It lets a friendly veil down on the lucent dark,
And not of any bright ground thing shows any spark.

Tomorrow's grey morning will show cow-parsley,
Hung all with shining drops, and the river will be
Duller because of the all soddenness of things,
Till the skylark breaks his reluctance, hangs shaking, and sings.

Edward Thomas

DIGGING

Today I think
Only with scents, – scents dead leaves yield,
And bracken, and wild carrot's seed,
And the square mustard field;

Odours that rise
When the spade wounds the root of tree,
Rose, currant, raspberry, or goutweed,
Rhubarb or celery;

The smoke's smell, too
Flowing from where a bonfire burns
The dead, the waste, the dangerous,
And all to sweetness turns.

It is enough
To smell, to crumble the dark earth,
While the robin sings over again
Sad songs of Autumn mirth.

Po Chü-I

PLANTING BAMBOOS

I am not suited for service in a country town;
At my closed door autumn grasses grow.
What could I do to ease a rustic heart?
I planted bamboos, more than a hundred shoots.
When I see their beauty, as they grow by the stream-side,
I feel again as though I lived in the hills,
And many a time when I have not much work
Round their railing I walk till night comes.
Do not say that their roots are still weak,
Do not say that their shade is still small;
Already I feel that both in courtyard and house
Day by day a fresher air moves.
But most I love lying near the window-side,
To hear in their branches the sound of the autumn wind.

Translated by Arthur Waley

Anyte

'LOUNGE IN THE SHADE OF THE LUXURIANT LAUREL'S'

Lounge in the shade of the luxuriant laurel's
beautiful foliage. And now drink sweet water
from the cold spring so that your limbs weary
with summer toil will find rest in the west wind.

Translated by Willis Barnstone

Contemplation

*'How can you realise the wideness
of the world?'*

Theodore Roethke

THE ROSE

1

There are those to whom place is unimportant,
But this place, where sea and fresh water meet,
Is important –
Where the hawks sway out into the wind,
Without a single wingbeat,
And the eagles sail low over the fir trees,
And the gulls cry against the crows
In the curved harbors,
And the tide rises up against the grass
Nibbled by sheep and rabbits.

A time for watching the tide,
For the heron's hieratic fishing,
For the sleepy cries of the towhee,
The morning birds gone, the twittering finches,
But still the flash of the kingfisher, the wingbeat of the scoter,
The sun a ball of fire coming down over the water,
The last geese crossing against the reflected afterlight,
The moon retreating into a vague cloud-shape
To the cries of the owl, the eerie whooper.
The old log subsides with the lessening waves,
And there is silence.

I sway outside myself
Into the darkening currents,
Into the small spillage of driftwood,
The waters swirling past the tiny headlands.
Was it here I wore a crown of birds for a moment
While on a far point of the rocks
The light heightened,
And below, in a mist out of nowhere,
The first rain gathered?

2

As when a ship sails with a light wind –
The waves less than the ripples made by rising fish,
The lacelike wrinkles of the wake widening, thinning out,
Sliding away from the traveler's eye,
The prow pitching easily up and down,
The whole ship rolling slightly sideways,
The stem high, dipping like a child's boat in a pond –
Our motion continues.

But this rose, this rose in the sea-wind,
Stays,
Stays in its true place,
Flowering out of the dark,
Widening at high noon, face upward,
A single wild rose, struggling out of the white embrace of the morning-
      glory,
Out of the briary hedge, the tangle of matted underbrush,
Beyond the clover, the ragged hay,
Beyond the sea pine, the oak, the wind-tipped madrona,
Moving with the waves, the undulating driftwood,
Where the slow creek winds down to the black sand of the shore
With its thick grassy scum and crabs scuttling back into their
      glistening craters.

And I think of roses, roses,
White and red, in the wide six-hundred-foot greenhouses,
And my father standing astride the cement benches,
Lifting me high over the four-foot stems, the Mrs Russells, and his
      own elaborate hybrids,
And how those flowerheads seemed to flow toward me, to beckon me,
      only a child, out of myself.

What need for heaven, then,
With that man, and those roses?

3

What do they tell us, sound and silence?
I think of American sounds in this silence:
On the banks of the Tombstone, the wind-harps having their say,
The thrush singing alone, that easy bird,
The killdeer whistling away from me,
The mimetic chortling of the catbird
Down in the corner of the garden, among the raggedy lilacs,
The bobolink skirring from a broken fencepost,
The bluebird, lover of holes in old wood, lilting its light song,
And that thin cry, like a needle piercing the ear, the insistent cicada,
And the ticking of snow around oil drums in the Dakotas,
The thin whine of telephone wires in the wind of a Michigan winter,
The shriek of nails as old shingles are ripped from the top of a roof,
The bulldozer backing away, the hiss of the sandblaster,
And the deep chorus of horns coming up from the streets in early
        morning.
I return to the twittering of swallows above water,
And that sound, that single sound,
When the mind remembers all,
And gently the light enters the sleeping soul,
A sound so thin it could not woo a bird,

Beautiful my desire, and the place of my desire.

I think of the rock singing, and light making its own silence,
At the edge of a ripening meadow, in early summer,
The moon lolling in the close elm, a shimmer of silver,
Or that lonely time before the breaking of morning
When the slow freight winds along the edge of the ravaged hillside,
And the wind tries the shape of a tree,
While the moon lingers,
And a drop of rain water hangs at the tip of a leaf
Shifting in the wakening sunlight
Like the eye of a new-caught fish.

4

I live with the rocks, their weeds,
Their filmy fringes of green, their harsh
Edges, their holes
Cut by the sea-slime, far from the crash
Of the long swell,
The oily, tar-laden walls
Of the toppling waves,
Where the salmon ease their way into the kelp beds,
And the sea rearranges itself among the small islands.

Near this rose, in this grove of sun-parched, wind-warped madronas,
Among the half-dead trees, I came upon the true ease of myself,
As if another man appeared out of the depths of my being,
And I stood outside myself,
Beyond becoming and perishing,
A something wholly other,
As if I swayed out on the wildest wave alive,
And yet was still.
And I rejoiced in being what I was:
In the lilac change, the white reptilian calm,
In the bird beyond the bough, the single one
With all the air to greet him as he flies,
The dolphin rising from the darkening waves;

And in this rose, this rose in the sea-wind,
Rooted in stone, keeping the whole of light,
Gathering to itself sound and silence –
Mine and the sea-wind's.

Pat Lowther

COAST RANGE

Just north of town
the mountains start to talk
back-of-the-head buzz
of high stubbled meadows
minute flowers
moss gravel and clouds

They're not snobs, these mountains,
they don't speak Rosicrucian,
they sputter with
billygoat-bearded creeks
bumsliding down
to splat into the sea

they talk with the casual
tongues of water
rising in trees

They're so humble they'll let you
blast highways through them
baring their iron and granite
sunset-coloured bones
broken for miles

And nights when
clouds foam on a beach
of clear night sky,
those high slopes creak
in companionable sleep

Move through gray green
aurora of rain
to the bare fact:
The land is bare.

Even the curly opaque Pacific
forest, chilling you full awake
with wet branch–slaps,
is somehow bare
stainless as sunlight:

The land is what's left
after the failure
of every kind of metaphor.

The plainness of first things
trees
gravel
rocks
naive root atom
of philosophy's first molecule

The mountains reject nothing
but can crack
open your mind
just by being intractably there

Atom: that which can not
be reduced

You can gut them
blast them
to slag
the shapes they've made in the sky
cannot be reduced

Po Chü-I

HAVING CLIMBED TO THE TOPMOST PEAK OF THE INCENSE-BURNER MOUNTAIN

Up and up, the Incense-burner Peak!
In my heart is stored what my eyes and ears perceived.
All the year – detained by official business;
Today at last I got a chance to go.
Grasping the creepers, I clung to dangerous rocks;
My hands and feet – weary with groping for hold.
There came with me three or four friends,
But two friends dared not go further.
At last we reached the topmost crest of the Peak;
My eyes were blinded, my soul rocked and reeled.
The chasm beneath me – ten thousand feet;
The ground I stood on, only a foot wide.
If you have not exhausted the scope of seeing and hearing,
How can you realise the wideness of the world?
The waters of the River looked narrow as a ribbon,
P'ên Castle smaller than a man's fist.
How it clings, the dust of the world's halter!
It chokes my limbs; I cannot shake it away.
Thinking of retirement, I heaved an envious sigh;
Then, with lowered head, came back to the Ants' Nest.

Translated by Arthur Waley

Sylvia Plath

ABOVE THE OXBOW

Here in this valley of discreet academies
We have not mountains, but mounts, truncated hillocks
To the Adirondacks, to northern Monadnock,
Themselves mere rocky hillocks to an Everest.
Still, they're our best mustering of height: by
Comparison with the sunken silver-grizzled
Back of the Connecticut, the river-level
Flats of Hadley farms, they're lofty enough
Elevations to be called something more than hills.
Green, wholly green, they stand their knobby spine
Against our sky: they are what we look southward to
Up Pleasant Street at Main. Poising their shapes
Between the snuff and red tar-paper apartments,
They mound a summer coolness in our view.

To people who live in the bottom of valleys
A rise in the landscape, hummock or hogback, looks
To be meant for climbing. A peculiar logic
In going up for the coming down if the post
We start at's the same post we finish by,
But it's the clear conversion at the top can hold
Us to the oblique road, in spite of a fitful
Wish for even ground, and it's the last cliff
Ledge will dislodge our cramped concept of space, unwall
Horizons beyond vision, spill vision
After the horizons, stretching the narrowed eye
To full capacity. We climb in hopes
Of such seeing up the leaf-shuttered escarpments,
Blindered by green, under a green-grained sky

Into the blue. Tops define themselves as places
Where nothing higher's to be looked to. Downward looks
Follow the black arrow-backs of swifts on their track
Of the air eddies' loop and arc though air's at rest
To us, since we see no leaf edge stir high
Here on a mount overlaid with leaves. The paint-peeled
Hundred-year-old hotel sustains its ramshackle
Four-way veranda, view-keeping above
The fallen timbers of its once remarkable
Funicular railway, witness to gone
Time, and to graces gone with the time. A state view-
Keeper collects half-dollars for the slopes
Of state scenery, sells soda, shows off viewpoints.
A ruddy skylight paints the gray oxbow

And paints the river's pale circumfluent stillness
As roses broach their carmine in a mirror. Flux
Of the desultory currents – all that unique
Stipple of shifting wave-tips is ironed out, lost
In the simplified orderings of sky –
Lorded perspectives. Maplike, the far fields are ruled
By correct green lines and no seedy free-for-all
Of asparagus heads. Cars run their suave
Colored beads on the strung roads, and the people stroll
Straightforwardly across the springing green.
All's peace and discipline down there. Till lately we
Lived under the shadow of hot rooftops
And never saw how coolly we might move. For once
A high hush quietens the crickets' cry.

Elizabeth Bishop

LESSON VI

What is Geography?
A description of the earth's surface.
What is the Earth?
The planet or body on which we live.
What is the shape of the Earth?
Round, like a ball.
Of what is the Earth's surface composed?
Land and water.

LESSON X

What is a Map?
A picture of the whole, or a part, of the
Earth's surface.
What are the directions on a Map?
Toward the top, North; toward the
bottom, South; to the right, East; to the
left, West.
In what direction from the center of the
picture is the Island?
North.
In what direction is the Volcano? The
Cape? The Bay? The Lake? The Strait?
The Mountains? The Isthmus?
What is in the East? In the West? In the
South? In the North? In the Northwest?
In the Southeast? In the Northeast?
In the Southwest?

[*From 'First Lessons in Geography,' Monteith's Geographical Series,*
A.S. Barnes & Co., 1884]

Rosemary Dobson

DRY RIVER

Scrabble of pencil marked it on the map.
The road, the blunt-nosed monster,
Thrust at the aching grasses blown the wind's way,
Shouldered fence-posts, ate up miles, exhaling
Dust and the stalks of grasses, smoke and thistles:
Riding its back I came to the Dry River.

It was my river. My spirit's destination.
Abstract of water, a dried depression,
Holed and bouldered and raked with fissures
Where the idea of water channelled
Irresistibly over and under
Endlessly forcing down to the sea.

It was my river by right of recognition.
Kindred and kith by its never-resting
Ever-longing scouring endeavour;
Carrying always the thought of water
From a lost spring dwindled to silence;
This is the burden of the Dry River.

Strange illusion that such a creek-bed
May seem to brim and shine at dew-fall,
Or ripple with shadow, or sound like water
With the cool, clear notes of the bell-birds' making.
Mirages deceive: I wait with longing
A flood of poems, a rain of rhyme.

Molly Holden

SO WHICH IS THE TRUTH?

Green and differences of green
and distances and depths of green
crowd the cool gardens, the leaves lax
in their avenues, the sun in a grey cloud;
all presences are motionless, unlit.

The cloud moves on, calls up
a sudden wind that pours itself over
the hedge with just-as-sudden
sunlight, reverses the leaves, stirs shadows,
fills the blown sky with a shrill
precipitate of martins. The tipped
kaleidoscope of colour balances.

A different garden.

So which is the truth?
which is the real garden?
the confusion of sunlight
or the grey moment's attitudes?

Liz Lochhead

INNER

I

make a change
if you get the weather

yes the place we're staying in
is green

bracken comes out clenched
only unbends
in the company of many others.
rigid, sinister as soldiers,
won't let us pass.

need not-English –
don't want to know the silly pretty names
for wildflowers
when I look them up in Sarah's book.
starlike in wiry grass
Skye flowers are too wild to call
Seapink   Kingcup   Lady's Smock.
another language.
last week on Lewis
Jim said he'd found that Gaelic words for colours
weren't colours as he thought he knew them.
chrome-yellow red-spectrum unsayable
straight from the tube.
rather a word might mean
red or reddish-brown earthbound.
another black or deep or purplish –
the colour of the darkness.
blue a clearness.
takes time says Jim
to know exactly how to paint here.
such distinctions.
'glàs'

might mean green or even calm-sea grey.
more a chroma of the weather
colour of the mind.

II

the birds
at first they bothered me
so big
so strange
their cries

just who
is that cuckoo
getting at all day?
the mechanical lark
on its yoyo string
the crossbow shadow of the hawk.

only took
two hooligan gulls
to chase that eagle round in circles
for half an hour before
they shot off yammering
to lord it at the tip.

big hoody
ugly bird
came down twice
sat square in the kitchen window
went caw caw
bashed his great horny beak twice hard
against the glass.

as if we were in an egg
big hoody was determined to smash.

but seems there's no omen in it.
hoodycrow's only

a bird
who's looking for a mate
and fallen for his own reflection

you know how people get.

III

mail comes
sometimes we send postcards
hope this finds you
we are much the same

midges very bad in evenings
we have woken every morning for a week
under the tin roof
listening to the rain
walking by the sea
we find clean bones
cork floats tiny
coral branches
green glass cockleshells
driftwood a broken
copper sprinkler rose gone green
and botched and oxidised
smooth pebbles mermaid purses
things to pick.
a collage on the windowledge.
I'd like
an art that could somehow marry
the washed-up manmade
and the wholly natural
make a change

don't even know
if I like cities or small places

heart urchin
rare to find an unbroken one
perfect from the sea
smaller
than a salt cellar
frail container
some marine-motif something
starlike etched on the shell
shake it   you can tell
something small and dry and shrivelled is inside.

shake it and your page
is seasoned with smithereens of sand

heart urchin
something to hold in your hand.

Pablo Neruda

OH EARTH, WAIT FOR ME

Return me, oh sun,
to my wild destiny,
rain of the ancient wood,
bring me back the aroma and the swords
that fall from the sky,
the solitary peace of pasture and rock,
the damp at the river-margins,
the smell of the larch tree,
the wind alive like a heart
beating in the crowded restlessness
of the towering araucaria.

Earth, give me back your pure gifts,
the towers of silence which rose
from the solemnity of their roots.
I want to go back to being what I have not been,
and learn to go back from such deeps
that amongst all natural things
I could live or not live; it does not matter
to be one stone more, the dark stone,
the pure stone which the river bears away.

Emily Dickinson

'"NATURE" IS WHAT WE SEE'

668

'Nature' is what we see—
The Hill—the Afternoon—
Squirrel—Eclipse—the Bumble bee—
Nay—Nature is Heaven—
Nature is what we hear—
The Boblink—the Sea—
Thunder—the Cricket—
Nay—Nature is Harmony—
Nature is what we know—
Yet have no art to say—
So impotent Our Wisdom is
To her Simplicity.

Goethe

EPIRRHEMA

Always in observing nature
Look at one and every creature;
Nothing's outside that's not within,
For nature has no heart or skin.
All at once that way you'll see
The sacred open mystery.

True seeming is the joy it gives,
The joy of serious playing;
No thing is single, if it lives,
But multiple its being.

Translated by Michael Hamburger

Rose Flint

CONNECTIONS

If I am aware, then the notes come;
I hear them – I suppose as bats do
or the broken-coated hound, whose eyes filter
something of earth's nature, whose eyes change
as he listens elsewhere. *Do you hear then?*
I ask him. *Is it Welsh rain coming to the garden,*
or something other? I only hear it through my hair,
the tips drink sound from silence.
Is this nectar then?
I imagine myself the humming-bird,
how this unchecked greenness would offer
hibiscus in the dog-rose, the wild sweetness
of some alien yellow juice
within the needled gooseberry or the stony pear.
The curlew bounces his song across the distance.
The hairs on my arm shudder with wind.
My dog hackles uneasy, he thinks
I am too near to the raven as it rises, croaking,
too near to the muttering self-involved tree
experimenting its blossom beyond us.
No, I say. Don't you see it?
The buzzard disturbs us, he is painting a circle
such as the mouth of a net, above us.
We are all in it. All.

Anne Finch

A NOCTURNAL REVERIE

In such a night, when every louder wind
Is to its distant cavern safe confined;
And only gentle Zephyr fans his wings,
And lonely Philomel, still waking, sings;
Or from some tree, famed for the owl's delight,
She, hollowing clear, directs the wanderer right;
In such a night, when passing clouds give place,

Or thinly veil the heaven's mysterious face;
When in some river overhung with green,
The waving moon and trembling leaves are seen;
When freshened grass now bears itself upright,
And makes cool banks to pleasing rest invite,
Whence springs the woodbind and the bramble-rose,
And where the sleepy cowslip sheltered grows;
Whilst now a paler hue the foxglove takes,
Yet chequers still with red the dusky brakes;
When scattered glow-worms, but in twilight fine,
Show trivial beauties, watch their hour to shine;
Whilst Salisb'ry stands the test of every light,
In perfect charms and perfect virtue bright;
When odours, which declined repelling day,
Through temperate air uninterrupted stray;
When darkened groves their softest shadows wear
And falling waters we distinctly hear;
When through the gloom more venerable shows
Some ancient fabric, awful in repose,
While sunburnt hills their swarthy looks conceal,
And swelling haycocks thicken up the vale;
When the loosed horse now, as his pasture leads,
Comes slowly grazing through th' adjoining meads,
Whose stealing pace and lengthened shade we fear,
Till torn-up forage in his teeth we hear;
When nibbling sheep at large pursue their food,
And unmolested kine rechew the cud;
When curlews cry beneath the village walls,
And to her straggling brood the partridge calls;
Their short-lived jubilee the creatures keep,
Which but endures whilst tyrant man does sleep;
When a sedate content the spirit feels,
And no fierce light disturbs, whilst it reveals,
But silent musings urge the mind to seek
Something too high for syllables to speak;
Till the free soul to a compos'dness charmed,
Finding the elements of rage disarmed,
O'er all below a solemn quiet grown,
Joys in th' inferior world and thinks it like her own:

In such a night let me abroad remain,
Till morning breaks, and all's confused again:
Our cares, our toils, our clamours are renewed,
Or pleasures, seldom reached, again pursued.

Elinor Wylie

WILD PEACHES

1

When the world turns completely upside down
You say we'll emigrate to the Eastern Shore
Aboard a river-boat from Baltimore;
We'll live among wild peach trees, miles from town,
You'll wear a coonskin cap, and I a gown
Homespun, dyed butternut's dark gold colour.
Lost, like your lotus-eating ancestor,
We'll swim in milk and honey till we drown.

The winter will be short, the summer long,
The autumn amber-hued, sunny and hot,
Tasting of cider and of scuppernong;
All seasons sweet, but autumn best of all.
The squirrels in their silver fur will fall
Like falling leaves, like fruit, before your shot.

2

The autumn frosts will lie upon the grass
Like bloom on grapes of purple-brown and gold.
The misted early mornings will be cold;
The little puddles will be roofed with glass.
The sun, which burns from copper into brass,
Melts these at noon, and makes the boys unfold
Their knitted mufflers; full as they can hold,
Fat pockets dribble chestnuts as they pass.

Peaches grow wild, and pigs can live in clover;
A barrel of salted herrings lasts a year;
The spring begins before the winter's over.
By February you may find the skins
Of garter snakes and water moccasins
Dwindled and harsh, dead-white and cloudy-clear.

3

When April pours the colours of a shell
Upon the hills, when every little creek
Is shot with silver from the Chesapeake
In shoals new-minted by the ocean swell,
When strawberries go begging, and the sleek
Blue plums lie open to the blackbird's beak,
We shall live well – we shall live very well.

The months between the cherries and the peaches
Are brimming cornucopias which spill
Fruits red and purple, sombre-bloomed and black;
Then, down rich fields and frosty river beaches
We'll trample bright persimmons, while you kill
Bronze partridge, speckled quail, and canvasback.

4

Down to the Puritan marrow of my bones
There's something in this richness that I hate.
I love the look, austere, immaculate,
Of landscapes drawn in pearly monotones.
There's something in my very blood that owns
Bare hills, cold silver on a sky of slate,
A thread of water, churned to milky spate
Streaming through slanted pastures fenced with stones.

I love those skies, thin blue or snowy gray,
Those fields sparse-planted, rendering meagre sheaves;
That spring, briefer than apple-blossom's breath,
Summer, so much too beautiful to stay,
Swift autumn, like a bonfire of leaves,
And sleepy winter, like the sleep of death.

Gillian Allnutt

SUNART

I remember the little disturbances of stone
our feet made there —

the call of the oyster-catchers
further along the shore —

the occasional car.
And if we were

careful, among the loch's accumulation of blue hills,
neither to close the soul completely

nor to break, by opening, that frail ligament
between the two halves of the ark

of any shell —
what were we listening for

as we held, still, the tiny wendletrap of April
in our cold wet hands?

A difficult hour. I remember the light
rain came ot of nowhere, silently

the salt on my lips
was there.

Ralph Waldo Emerson

HAMATREYA

Bulkeley, Hunt, Willard, Hosmer, Meriam, Flint,
Possessed the land which rendered to their toil
Hay, corn, roots, hemp, flax, apples, wool and wood.
Each of these landlords walked amidst his farm,
Saying, 'Tis mine, my children's and my name's.
How sweet the west wind sounds in my own trees!
How graceful climb those shadows on my hill!
I fancy these pure waters and the flags
Know me, as does my dog: we sympathize;
And, I affirm, my actions smack of the soil.'

Where are these men? Asleep beneath their grounds:
And strangers, fond as they, their furrows plough.
Earth laughs in flowers, to see her boastful boys
Earth-proud, proud of the earth which is not theirs
Who steer the plough, but cannot steer their feet
Clear of the grave.

They added ridge to valley, brook to pond,
And sighed for all that bounded their domain;
'This suits me for a pasture; that's my park;
We must have clay, lime, gravel, granite-ledge,
And misty lowland, where to go for peat.
The land is well – lies fairly to the south.
'Tis good, when you have crossed the sea and back,
To find the sitfast acres where you left them.'

Ah! the hot owner sees not Death, who adds
Him to his land, a lump of mold the more.
Hear what the Earth says:

EARTH-SONG

'Mine and yours;
Mine, not yours.
Earth endures;
Stars abide –

Shine down in the old sea;
Old are the shores;
But where are old men?
I who have seen much,
Such have I never seen.

'The lawyer's deed
Ran sure,
In tail,
To them, and to their heirs
Who shall succeed,
Without fail,
Forevermore.

'Here is the land,
Shaggy with wood,
With its old valley,
Mound and flood.
But the heritors?
Fled like the flood's foam.
The lawyer, and the laws,
And the kingdom,
Clean swept herefrom.

'They called me theirs,
Who so controlled me;
Yet every one
Wished to stay, and is gone,
How am I theirs,
If they cannot hold me,
But I hold them?'

When I heard the Earth-song,
I was no longer brave;
My avarice cooled
Like lust in the chill of the grave.

J. Kitchener Davies

From THE SOUND OF THE WIND THAT IS BLOWING

The land of Y Llain was on the high marsh   *the strip*
on the border between Caron-is-Clawdd and Padarn Odwyn
Slanting from Cae Top down to Y Waun,   *top field, the moor field*
and beyond Cae Top was a glade of dark trees –
pines and tall larches – to break the cold wind,
the wind from the north.
And there were the small four-sided fields
like a checkerboard, or a patchwork quilt,
and around each of the fields, a hedge.

   My father planted the hedges farthest from the house, –
the hedges of Cae Top and Cae Brwyn –   *field of the rushes*
myself a youngster at his heels
putting the plants in his hand:
three hawthorns and a beech-tree,
three hawthorns and a beech-tree in turn;
his feet measuring the distance between them along
    the top of the ditch,
squeezing them solidly into the loose earth-and-chalk.
Then the patterned wiring outside them –
the square posts of peeled oak-wood
sunk deep in the living earth –
and I getting to turn the wiring-engine on the post
while he did the stapling,
the hammer ringing in my ears with the pounding.
And I daring on the sly
to send a telegram back over the taut wires
to the other children at the far end of the ditch,
the note of music raising its pitch
with each turn I gave the old wiring-engine's handle.
   My grandfather, said my father, had planted the Middle Fields – Cae
     Cwteri, Cae Polion, Cae Troi –   *Ditch field, post field, turning field*
but generations we knew nothing at all about,
except for the mark of their handiwork on
Cae Lloi and Cae Moch,   *field of the calves, field of the pigs*
had planted the tall strong stout-trunked trees round the house,

and set sweet-plums here and there in the hedges.
     And there we children would be
safe in a fold in the ditch under the hedges,
the dried leaves a coverlet to keep us warm
(like the babes in the story hidden with leaves by the birds).
The breeze that trickled through the trunks of the hedges
was not enough to ruffle the wren's and the robin's feathers:
but above the hedges and the trees, above the house,
aloft in the firmament, the wind was
tumbling the clouds, tickling them till their white laughter
was unruly hysteria like children on a kitchen floor,
till the excess of play turns suddenly strange
and the laughter's whiteness scowls, and darkens,
and the tears burst forth, and the clouds escape
in a race from the wind, from the tickling and the tumbling,
escaping headlong from the wind's provocation –
the pursuing wind outside me,
and I fast in the fold in the ditch beneath the leaves
listening to its sound, outside,
with nothing at all occurring within what I am
because of the care and craft of generations of my fathers
planting their hedges prudently to shelter me in my day, –
nothing – despite my wishing and wishing.

Charles Tomlinson

AT STOKE

I have lived in a single landscape. Every tone
   And turn have had for their ground
These beginnings in grey-black: a land
   Too handled to be primary – all the same,
The first in feeling. I thought it once
   Too desolate, diminished and too tame
To be the foundation for anything. It straggles
   A haggard valley and lets through
Discouraged greennesses, lights from a pond or two.
   By ash-tips, or where the streets give out
In cindery in-betweens, the hills
   Swell up and free of it to where, behind
The whole vapoury, patched battlefield,
   The cows stand steaming in an acrid wind.
This place, the first to seize on my heart and eye,
   Has been their hornbook and their history.

Czeslaw Milosz

ADVICE

Yes, it is true that the landscape changed a little.
Where there were forests, now there are pears of
   factories, cisterns.
Approaching the mouth of the river we hold our noses.
Its current carries oil and chlorine and methyl com-
   pounds,
Not to mention the by-products of the Books of Ab-
   straction:
Excrement, urine, and dead sperm.
A huge stain of artificial colour poisons fish in the sea.
Where the shore of the bay was overgrown with rushes
Now it is rusted with smashed machines, ashes and
   bricks.
We used to read in old poets about the scent of earth
And grasshoppers. Now we bypass the fields:

Ride as fast as you can through the chemical zone of the
    farmers.
The insect and the bird are extinguished. Far away a
    bored man
Drags dust with his tractor, an umbrella against the sun.
What do we regret? – I ask. A tiger? A shark?
We created a second Nature in the image of the first
So as not to believe that we live in Paradise.
It is possible that when Adam woke in the garden
The beasts licked the air and yawned, friendly,
While their fangs and their tails, lashing their backs,
Were figurative and the red-backed shrike,
Later, much later, named Lanius collurio,
Did not impale caterpillars on spikes of the blackthorn.
However, other than that moment, what we know of
    Nature
Does not speak in its favour. Ours is no worse.
So I beg you, no more of those lamentations.

Amy Clampitt

THE REEDBEDS OF THE HACKENSACK

Scummed maunderings that nothing loves but reeds
Phragmites, neighbors of the greeny asphodel
that thrive among the windings of the Hackensack,
collaborating to subvert the altogether ugly
though too down-to-earth to be quite fraudulent:
what's landfill but the backside of civility?

Dreckpot, the Styx and Malebolge of civility,
brushed by the fingering plumes of beds and reeds:
Manhattan's moat of stinks, the rancid asphodel
aspiring from the gradually choking Hackensack,
ring-ditch inferior to the vulgar, the mugly ugly,
knows-no-better, fake but not quite fraudulent:

what's scandal but the candor of the fraudulent?
Miming the burnish of a manicured civility,
the fluent purplings of uncultivated reeds,
ex post cliché survivors like the asphodel,
drink, as they did the Mincius, the Hackensack
in absent-minded benediction on the merely ugly.

Is there a poetry of the incorrigibly ugly,
free of all furbishings that mark it fraudulent?
When toxins of an up-against-the-wall civility
have leached away the last patina of these reeds,
and promised landfill, with its lethal asphodel
of fumes, blooms the slow dying of the Hackensack,

shall I compare thee, Mincius, to the Hackensack?
Now Italy knows how to make its rivers ugly,
must, ergo, all such linkages be fraudulent,
gilding the laureate hearse of a defunct civility?
Smooth-sliding Mincius, crowned with vocal reeds,
coevals of that greeny local weed the asphodel,

that actual, unlettered entity the asphodel,
may I, among the channels of the Hackensack –
those Edens-in-the-works of the irrevocably ugly,
where any mourning would of course be fraudulent –
invoke the scrannel ruth of a forsooth civility,
the rathe, the deathbed generations of these reeds?

Molly Holden

PIECES OF UNPROFITABLE LAND

The pieces of unprofitable land
are what I like, best seen in winter,
triangular tail of cottage garden
tall with dead willowherb, and tangled splinter
of uncut copse edging the red-ploughed fields,
and between hedge and headland of such fields
the slope of one-in-four the plough can't touch,
mayweed and old larks' nests its only yields.

In countryside so arable and fenced
that verges are the only common land
these roughs are memories of former wilds
untouched by foot, unharvested by hand.
Attained by sight alone, because so small,
private, or thorny, stuffed with the years' seeds,
their failure's proof of reclamation,
their vigour justifies all wastes and weeds.

Mary Ursula Bethell

PAUSE

When I am very earnestly digging
I lift my head sometimes, and look at the mountains,
And muse upon them, muscles relaxing.

I think how freely the wild grasses flower there,
How grandly the storm-shaped trees are massed in their gorges
And the rain-worn rocks strewn in magnificent heaps.

Pioneer plants on those uplands find their own footing;
No vigorous growth, there, is an evil weed:
All weathers are salutary.

It is only a little while since this hillside
Lay untrammelled likewise,
Unceasingly swept by transmarine winds.

In a very little while, it may be,
When our impulsive limbs and our superior skulls
Have to the soil restored several ounces of fertiliser,

The Mother of all will take charge again,
And soon wipe away with her elements
Our small fond human enclosures.

Sheenagh Pugh

GEOGRAPHY 2

The land wrote itself before any
came to chart it: continents broke
and reassembled; two masses crashed
and threw a mountain range, a border
waiting for customs posts; glaciers cut
narrow valleys, close and separate,
each shuttered cautiously from its neighbour.
A coast curved itself into a haven
for shipping; a hill kept watch
on the landscape till the fort was built.
A river spread rich gentle living
over these fields; elsewhere, the want
of water made the contours stand out
like starved bones.

   And when it was all ready
they came, at last, to be masters
of it all; to take up the lives
mapped out for them.

Alice Walker

ON SIGHT

I am so thankful I have seen
The Desert
And the creatures in The Desert
And the desert Itself.

The Desert has its own moon
Which I have seen
With my own eye

There is no flag on it.

Trees of the desert have arms
All of which are always up
That is because the moon is up
The sun is up
Also the sky
The stars
Clouds
None with flags.

If there were flags, I doubt
The trees would point.
Would you?

Angelina Weld Grimké

THE BLACK FINGER

I have just seen a beautiful thing
        Slim and still,
Against a gold, gold sky
        A straight cypress,
        Sensitive,
        Exquisite,
A black finger
Pointing upwards.
Why, beautiful, still finger are you black?
And why are you pointing upwards?

Adrienne Rich

RURAL REFLECTIONS

This is the grass your feet are planted on.
You paint it orange or you sing it green,
        But you have never found
A way to make the grass mean what you mean.

A cloud can be whatever you intend:
Ostrich or leaning tower or staring eye.
        But you have never found
A cloud sufficient to express the sky.

Get out there with your splendid expertise;
Raymond who cuts the meadow does no less.
        Inhuman nature says:
Inhuman patience is the true success.

Human impatience trips you as you run;
        Stand still and you must lie.
Is is the grass that cuts the mower down;
It is the cloud that swallows up the sky.

Hans Magnus Enzensberger

LACHESIS LAPPONICA

here it is bright, by the rusty water, nowhere. here,
these are the grey willows, this is the grey grass,
this is the dusky bright sky, here i stand.

(*that is no standpoint*, says the bird in my head.)

here where i stand, that whiteness in the wind is the moor
    sedge,
look how it flickers, the silent empty wilderness here is the
    earth.

(*¡viva!* cries the dusky bird: *¡viva fidel castro!*)

what's castro got to do with it (*what have you got to do
    with it,
with the cotton grass, the hair grass by the dusky water?*)

nothing, i've nothing, bird, do you hear? and no bird,
bird, whistles for me. (*that is true.*) leave me in peace.
here i'm not fighting. (it's a curlew, most likely.)

over there is north, where it's getting dark, you see,
the moor gets dark very slowly. here i have nothing,
here i have nothing to do. the whiteness up in the north
is the spirits of the north, the moor's bright spirits.

(*that is no standpoint, those are no spirits,
those are birch trees*, it shrieks, *here nothing happens.*)

that's good. i'm not fighting. leave me. i'm waiting.

in time, very slowly, the bark peels off,
(*it's nothing to me*) and the whiteness there,
the whiteness there under the whiteness, you see,
that i shall read. (*and here*, it says, *the exact time:
twenty-three fifty.*) here, in the rusty moss.

i believe in spirits (*there's no such thing!*) empty silent
wild.

i too am a spirit. and so is that shrieking bird
in my silent head. (*don't say that.*)

you both look northward. midnight. (*on times square
you stand, dead man, i know you, i see you buy,
sell and be sold, it is you, on red square,
on the kurfürstendamm, and you look at your rusty watch.*)

(it's a curlew, most likely, or else a peewit.
don't say that, get it out of your head.)

i'll cut off your head, bird. (*it's your own.*
(¡*viva fidel! better dead than red. have a break! ban the bomb!
über alles in der welt!*) don't say that. (*you are all that,*
says the bird, *imagine, you have been that, you are that.*)

how do you mean that? (*in all seriousness*, says the bird and
    laughs.)
a curlew can't laugh. (*it's yourself*, it says,
who are laughing. you'll regret it. i know who you are,
death's head on the kurfürstendamm.) on the moor.

white, dusky, grey. there are no victories here.
that is the moor sedge, those are the grey willows,
that is the bright bird against the dusky sky.

now it is midnight, now the bark splits,
(*the exact time:*) it is white, (*zero two minutes*)
there in the mist, where it's getting dark, you can read it,
the blank page, the silent empty wilderness.
here nothing happens. (*don't say that.*) here i am.
leave me. (*don't say that.*) leave me alone.

(*do you agree with me, death's head, and are you dead?*
is it a peewit? if you are not dead
what are you waiting for?) i'm waiting. i'm waiting.

it is on the outermost edge of this plain, marsh grass,
cotton grass, hair grass, where it is dusky already, bird,
(*how do you mean?*) do you see? do you see the white script?

(*coward*, it says, *good luck. we shall meet again.*)
leave me where all is blank. (*death's head.*)
look how it flickers. (and the dusky bird
in my head says to itself: *he's asleep, that means*
he agrees.)
                but i am not asleep.

                                    Translated by Michael Hamburger

[In 1732 Carl von Linné went on an expedition to
Lapland. His account of the journey appeared
posthumously in England under the title *Lachesis*
Lapponica (1811). It is regarded as the definitive
description of this region.]

Sylvia Plath

TWO CAMPERS IN CLOUD COUNTRY

(Rock Lake, Canada)

In this country there is neither measure nor balance
To redress the dominance of rocks and woods,
The passage, say, of these man-shaming clouds.

No gesture of yours or mine could catch their attention,
No word make them carry water or fire the kindling
Like local trolls in the spell of a superior being.

Well, one wearies of the Public Gardens: one wants a vacation
Where trees and clouds and animals pay no notice;
Away from the labeled elms, the tame tea-roses.

It took three days driving north to find a cloud
The polite skies over Boston couldn't possibly accommodate.
Here on the last frontier of the big, brash spirit

The horizons are too far off to be chummy as uncles;
The colors assert themselves with a sort of vengeance.
Each day concludes in a huge splurge of vermilions

And night arrives in one gigantic step.
It is comfortable, for a change, to mean so little.
These rocks offer no purchase to herbage or people:

They are conceiving a dynasty of perfect cold.
In a month we'll wonder what plates and forks are for.
I lean to you, numb as a fossil. Tell me I'm here.

The Pilgrims and Indians might never have happened.
Planets pulse in the lake like bright amoebas;
The pines blot our voices up in their lightest sighs.

Around our tent the old simplicities sough
Sleepily as Lethe, trying to get in.
We'll wake blank-brained as water in the dawn.

Wallace Stevens

THIS SOLITUDE OF CATARACTS

He never felt twice the same about the flecked river,
Which kept flowing and never the same way twice, flowing

Through many places, as if it stood still in one,
Fixed like a lake on which the wild ducks fluttered,

Ruffling its common reflections, thought-like Monadnocks.
There seemed to be an apostrophe that was not spoken.

There was so much that was real that was not real at all.
He wanted to feel the same way over and over.

He wanted the river to go on flowing the same way,
To keep on flowing. He wanted to walk beside it,

Under the buttonwoods, beneath a moon nailed fast.
He wanted his heart to stop beating and his mind to rest

In a permanent realization, without any wild ducks
Or mountains that were not mountains, just to know how it
    would be,

Just to know how it would feel, released from destruction,
To be a bronze man breathing under archaic lapis,

Without the oscillations of planetary pass-pass,
Breathing his bronzen breath at the azury centre of time.

Observation

'Sensitive to the millionth of a flicker'

Hsü Ling

THE WATERS OF LUNG-T'OU

(The North-West Frontier)

The road that I came by mounts eight thousand feet;
The river that I crossed hangs a hundred fathoms.
The brambles so thick that in summer one cannot pass;
The snow so high that in winter one cannot climb!
With branches that interlace Lung Valley is dark;
Against cliffs that tower one's voice beats and echoes.
I turn my head, and it seems only a dream
That I ever lived in the streets of Hsien-yang.

Translated by Arthur Waley

Norman MacCaig

SIGNS AND SIGNALS

The Loch of the Wolf's Pass
And the Loch of the Green Corrie
Are both hung high in the air.
Rock, sphagnum and grass

Set them there. They shine
With the drenched light of the sky.
Round them the deer: and, over,
An eagle rules its line

Straight for its nest, midge-speck
On a ledge of Ben More Assynt –
Ptarmigan crouch in the stones . . .
Now the hinds move off, on trek

To Glen Coul; they unhurriedly wind
Round the Loch of the Green Corrie
And the Loch of the Wolf's Pass
That are hung there in my mind

And drenched with meaning – where the high
Eagle tears apart
The wind, and the ptarmigan, each
A stone with a crimson eye,

Crouch on my self's ground.
The water rocks, and the meaning
Tilts to its brighter self
And flashes all worlds around –

I see them jump in the air,
They wheel in the tall cathedral
Where space tumbles before
The altar of everywhere.

Les A. Murray

From FOUR GAELIC POEMS
3. THE GUM FOREST

After the last gapped wire on a post,
homecoming for me, to enter the gum forest.

This old slow battlefield: parings of armour,
cracked collars, elbows, scattered on the ground.

New trees step out of old: lemon and ochre
splitting out of grey everywhere, in the gum forest.

In there for miles, shade track and ironbark slope,
depth casually beginning all around, at a little distance.

Sky sifting, and always a hint of smoke in the light;
you can never reach the heart of the gum forest.

In here is like a great yacht harbour, charmed to leaves,
innumerable tackle, poles wrapped in spattered sail,
or an unknown army in reserve for centuries.

Flooded-gums on creek ground, each tall because of each.
Now a blackbutt in bloom is showering with bees
but warm blood sleeps in the middle of the day.
The witching hour is noon in the gum forest.

Foliage builds like a layering splash: ground water
drily upheld in edge-on, wax-rolled, gall-puckered
leaves upon leaves. The shoal life of parrots up there.

Stone footings, trunk-shattered. Non-human lights. Enormous
abandoned machines. The mysteries of the gum forest.

Delight to me, though, at the water-smuggling creeks,
health to me, too, under banksia candles and combs.

A wind is up, rubbing limbs above the bullock roads;
mountains are waves in the ocean of the gum forest.

I go my way, looking back sometimes, looking round me,
singed oils clear my mind, and the pouring sound high up.

Why have I denied the passions of my time? To see
lightning strike upward out of the gum forest.

Emily Dickinson

'BLAZING IN GOLD'

Blazing in Gold and quenching in Purple.
Leaping like Leopards to the Sky
Then at the feet of the Old Horizon
Laying her spotted Face to die
Stooping as low as the Otter's Window
Touching the Roof and tinting the Barn
Kissing her Bonnet to the Meadow
And the Juggler of Day is gone

John Pepper Clark

IBADAN

Ibadan,
            running splash of rust
and gold – flung and scattered
among seven hills like broken
china in the sun.

C.P. Cavafy

MORNING SEA

Let me stop here. Let me, too, look at nature awhile.
The brilliant blue of the morning sea, of the cloudless sky,
the shore yellow; all lovely,
all bathed in light.

Let me stand here. And let me pretend I see all this
(I actually did see it for a minute when I first stopped)
and not my usual day-dreams here too,
my memories, those sensual images.

Eldred Revett

LAND-SCHAP BETWEEN TWO HILLS

Plac'd on yon' fair though beetle brow
That on the pleasures frowns below,
Let us with sprightly phancie thence
Teach the dumb Rhetorik Eloquence;
And leave the Painters Art out-gone,
Inliv'ning by transcription.
    First then observe with levell'd sight
A rising to this opposite;
As if the wind in billow drave
Here, and had rowld the earth in wave:
The Aspen and the Bramble heaves
And a white foam froth's in the leaves:

That spot beneath, that lies so plain
Schorch'd here and there, hath lost the grain:
As Sol there dried the Beams he swet
And stain'd the grass-green coverlet;
That Goat the bushes nigh doth browse
Seems the un-ravell'd plush to frowse;
And now let fall the eye it sees
A pretty storm of clowdy trees,
To us seem black and full of rain,
As they would scatter in the plain:
From hence the hill declineth spent,
With imperceptible descent,
'Till un-awares abroad it flow
Lost in the deluge spreads below.
   An Age-bow'd oak doth under-root
As it would prostrate at its foot;
Whose thrown-out arms in length display
And a fair shady carpet lay;
On it a lad in russet coat
His soul melts through the vocal oate;
And near that black eyed Nymph doth draw
As if her eyes hung on the straw:
The scrip and leathern Bottle nigh,
(With guardian too *Melampo*) lie:
The flocks are round about them spread
In num'rous fleece have clad the Meade;
And now our eyes but weakly see
Quite tippled with varietie:
Here the grass rowls, and hills between
Stud it with little tufts of green:
There in the midst a tree doth stray
Escap'd, as it had lost the way,
And a winding river steals
That with it self drunk curling reels,
A cheaper flood than *Tagus* goes
And with dissolved silver flowes.
Some way the field thence swells at ease
And lifts our sight up by degrees
To where the steep side dissie lies

Supinely fast in precipice
Till with the bank oppos'd it lie,
In a proportion'd Harmonie,
As Nature here did sit and sing,
About the *cradle* of the spring.

Elizabeth Bishop

THE BIGHT

(*On my birthday*)

At low tide like this how sheer the water is.
White, crumbling ribs of marl protrude and glare
and the boats are dry, the pilings dry as matches.
Absorbing, rather than being absorbed,
the water in the bight doesn't wet anything,
the color of the gas flame turned as low as possible.
One can smell it turning to gas; if one were Baudelaire
one could probably hear it turning to marimba music.
The little ocher dredge at work off the end of the dock
already plays the dry perfectly off-beat claves.
The birds are outsize. Pelicans crash
into this peculiar gas unnecessarily hard,
it seems to me, like pickaxes,
rarely coming up with anything to show for it,
and going off with humorous elbowings.
Black-and-white man-of-war birds soar
on impalpable drafts
and open their tails like scissors on the curves
or tense them like wishbones, till they tremble.
The frowsy sponge boats keep coming in
with the obliging air of retrievers,
bristling with jackstraw gaffs and hooks
and decorated with bobbles of sponges.
There is a fence of chicken wire along the dock
where, glinting like little plowshares,
the blue-gray shark tails are hung up to dry
for the Chinese-restaurant trade.
Some of the little white boats are still piled up
against each other, or lie on their sides, stove in,
and not yet salvaged, if they ever will be, from the last bad storm,
like torn-open, unanswered letters.
The bight is littered with old correspondences.
Click. Click. Goes the dredge,
and brings up a dripping jawful of marl.
All the untidy activity continues,
awful but cheerful.

Elizabeth Coatsworth

WHALE AT TWILIGHT

The sea is enormous, but calm with evening
    and sunset,
rearranging its islands for the night,
    changing its own blues,
smoothing itself against the rocks, without
    playfulness, without thought.
No stars are out, only sea birds flying to
    distant reefs.
No vessels intrude, no lobstermen haul their
    pots.
Only somewhere out toward the horizon a thin
    column of water appears
and disappears again, and then rises once more,
tranquil as a fountain in a garden where no
    wind blows.

R.S. Thomas

NIGHT AND MORNING

(From the Welsh Traditional)

One night of tempest I arose and went
Along the Menai shore on dreaming bent;
The wind was strong, and savage swung the tide,
And the waves blustered on Caernarfon side.

But on the morrow, when I passed that way,
On Menai shore the hush of heaven lay;
The wind was gentle and the sea a flower,
And the sun slumbered on Caernarfon tower.

Pablo Neruda

THE NIGHT IN ISLA NEGRA

The ancient night and the unruly salt
beat at the walls of my house;
lonely is the shadow, the sky
by now is a beat of the ocean,
and sky and shadow explode
in the fray of unequal combat;
all night long they struggle,
nobody knows the weight
of the harsh clarity that will go on opening
like a languid fruit;
thus is born on the coast,
out of turbulent shadow, the hard dawn,
nibbled by the salt in movement,
swept up by the weight of night,
bloodstained in its marine crater.

Translated by Alastair Reid

Tomas Tranströmer

FROM MARCH '79

Tired of all who come with words, words but no language
I went to the snow-covered island.
The wild does not have words.
The unwritten pages spread themselves out in all
                    directions!
I come across the marks of roe-deer's hooves in the
                    snow.
Language but no words.

Translated by John F. Deane

Alice Sadongei

WHAT FRANK, MARTHA AND I KNOW ABOUT THE DESERT

My mother
used to speak about Coyote.
She talked to Praying Mantis –
asked him
when rain was coming.
She taught me, Frank and Martha
to look for sap
on the greasy bark
of mesquite.
(the sap has crunchy, crystalled edges, a smooth, wax-like center)
She told us
how to eat mesquite beans.
'gnaw on the ends, don't eat the seeds'
(the fiber inside the pod is sweet)
On zoo visits
we'd hear tales of Coyote.
'Coyote fell on desert sand
blinded by his vanity. Bluebird
laughed at him – now his coat is streaked and blotched.'
Coyote knew
we were talking about him.
He'd let us look into his eyes.
My mother
would take me, Frank and Martha
to the desert in spring.
'Stand
alone out here.
Don't speak.
Listen
to the desert.'

My mother
showed us a purple desert flower
that looked like a rabbit.
(they grow near the highway)
There are patches of poppies
near my grandfather's village.
> Out there
> in the desert
> where there is nothing
> but heat and the wobbly
> shade of the mesquite
> tree, look around before
> you sit on a rock. There
> may be lizards or snakes⁻
> sleeping under the cool
> stone.

Anon [Yoruba]

RIDDLES

We call the dead – they answer.
We call the living – they do not answer.
  [*leaves*]

A round calabash in the spear grass.
  [*moon and stars*]

A thin staff reaches from heaven to earth.
  [*rain*]

The bereaved one has stopped weeping.
The compassionate friend is still crying.
  [*rain and the dripping leaves after rain*]

A pile of shit on a leaf, and covered with a leaf.
  [*humanity between heaven and earth*]

Anon [Mudbara★]

'THE DAY BREAKS'

The day breaks – the first rays of the rising Sun, stretching
   her arms.
Daylight breaking, as the Sun rises to her feet,
Sun rising, scattering the darkness, lighting up the land
With disk shining, bringing daylight, lighting up the
   land . . .
People are moving about, talking, feeling the warmth,
Burning through the gorge she rises, walking westwards,
Wearing her waistband of human hair.
She shines on the blossoming coolibah tree, with its sprawling
   roots.
Its shady branches spreading.

★ A tribe of Wave Hill, northern Australia

Rosario Morales

¡ROBLES, M'HIJA, ROBLES!

What is the name of the tree that blossoms in the
   subtropical spring
When the coffee blooms white and heavy with scent
   on the long low dark branches,
The tree that lined the roads in the mountains
   shedding lilac petals onto the wet black tarmac
Wet from the hard spring rains that knocked the blossoms
   off their branches with their huge heavy drops
Knocked the coffee blooms with the delicate light
   purple petals off the tall tree
The tree reflected in the rain-washed road,
What is the name of the tree?

Robert Bly

DRIVING TOWARD THE LAC QUI PARLE RIVER

I

I am driving; it is dusk; Minnesota.
The stubble field catches the last growth of sun.
The soybeans are breathing on all sides.
Old men are sitting before their houses on carseats
In the small towns. I am happy,
The moon rising above the turkey sheds.

II

The small world of the car
Plunges through the deep fields of the night,
On the road from Willmar to Milan.
This solitude covered with iron
Moves through the fields of night
Penetrated by the noise of crickets.

III

Nearly to Milan, suddenly a small bridge.
And water kneeling in the moonlight.
In small towns the houses are built right on the ground;
The lamplight falls on all fours in the grass.
When I reach the river, the full moon covers it;
A few people are talking low in a boat.

Gary Snyder

THE TRAIL IS NOT A TRAIL

I drove down the Freeway
And turned off at an exit
And went along a highway
Til it came to a sideroad
Drove up the sideroad
Til it turned to a dirt road
Full of bumps, and stopped.
Walked up a trail
But the trail got rough
And it faded away –
Out in the open,
Everywhere to go.

Olga Broumas

ROADSIDE

Old fir young fir
afternoon indiscriminate
cloudy hard to time
stop the car on dirt
road stretch head
towards the sound of river
oblivious still from the high
way speed sweet sound of river
incessant rising through my ears
eyes I'm clear
across the clearing
before I know the wind
is rising in the branches
not the river very cold
wind very dry
no grass or undergrowth
young pine sparse between old pine
dead branches
all the way across
a path I had been crushing
riblike winter-polished twigs
bone dry

Seamus Heaney

THE ROAD AT FROSSES

Not an avenue and not a bower.
For a quarter-mile or so, where the county road
Is running straight across North Antrim bog,

Tall old fir trees line it on both sides.
Scotch firs, that is. Calligraphic shocks
Bushed and tufted in prevailing winds.

You drive into a meaning made of trees.
Or not exactly trees. It is a sense
Of running through and under without let,

Of glimpse and dapple. A life all trace and skim
The car has vanished out of. A fanned nape
Sensitive to the millionth of a flicker.

Emily Dickinson

'AS IMPERCEPTIBLY AS GRIEF'

As imperceptibly as Grief
The Summer lapsed away –
Too imperceptible at last
To seem like Perfidy –
A Quietness distilled
As Twilight long begun,
Or Nature spending with herself
Sequestered Afternoon –
The Dusk drew earlier in –
The Morning foreign shone –
A courteous, yet harrowing Grace,
As Guest, that would be gone –
And thus, without a Wing
Or service of a Keel
Our Summer made her light escape
Into the Beautiful.

Laury Wells

THE NOMADS

The night draws in with the setting sun
And shadows very long,
A slight breeze stirs through the grass and burrs
Like the note of a mournful song.

And the dingos howl in the mulga scrub
In search of a water hole,
And wurleys gleam from shining beams
Off a rising moon of gold.

A dead snake sways from a broken limb
As figures move around,
By the fire's and moonbeams' rays
The nomads settle down.

Edith Södergran

NOCTURNE

Moonlit evening, silver clear
and the night's blue billows,
sparkling waves, numberless,
follow one another.
Shadows fall along the path,
on the shore the bushes softly weep,
black giants guard its silver in their keep.
Silence deep in summer's midst,
sleep and dream, –
the moon glides out across the sea
white tender gleam.

Anon [Ewe]

THE SKY

The sky at night is like a big city
where beasts and men abound,
but never once has anyone
killed a fowl or a goat,
and no bear has ever killed a prey.
There are no accidents; there are no losses.
Everything knows its way.

Translated by Kafu Hob

Disquiet

'Something warns me everywhere'

Ruth Fainlight

THE POWER SOURCE

In this part of the country
all through July, sometimes
round the clock, after
the first crop's cut and stacked,
the rape-seed brought inside
that new blue corrugated
plastic barn behind
the churchyard, the driers keep blowing.
Industrial farming. Often
annoying, ignored, it fades into
the background; one more factor
in the ambient pattern of sound.

I can let it lower my guard
and mood – becoming sulky,
agitated – or get me
high on the idea of progress:
a theme to brood on. Either
way, stimulated or
nerve-racked, I find the summer
different than before
I noticed the strain of trying
to be a nature-poet
these unbucolic days.
The power source has shifted.

When it stops, though other
motors seem much louder:
passing tourist traffic,
helicopters spraying,
tractors (drivers earphoned
to muffle their own noise),
the vital note is missing.
I wait its starting-up,
knowing I'll be uneasy
in the interval
between now and the August
combine-harvesters.

Gillian Clarke

NEIGHBOURS

That spring was late. We watched the sky
and studied charts for shouldering isobars.
Birds were late to pair. Crows drank from the lamb's
    eye.

Over Finland small birds fell: song-thrushes
steering north, smudged signatures on light,
migrating warblers, nightingales.

Wing-beats failed over fjords, each lung a sip of gall.
Children were warned of their dangerous beauty.
Milk was spilt in Poland. Each quarrel

the blowback from some old story,
a mouthful of bitter air from the Ukraine
brought by the wind out of its box of sorrows.

This spring a lamb sips caesium on a Welsh hill.
A child, lifting her face to drink the rain,
takes into her blood the poisoned arrow.

Now we are all neighbourly, each little town
in Europe twinned to Chernobyl, each heart
with the burnt fireman, the child on the Moscow train.

In the democracy of the virus and the toxin
we wait. We watch for bird migrations,
one bird returning with green in its voice,

glasnost,
golau glas,
a first break of blue.

[*golau glas: blue light*]

Helen Dunmore

PERMAFROST

For all frozen things –
my middle finger that whitens
from its old, ten-minute frostbite,

for black, slimy potatoes
left in the clamp,
for darkness and cold like cloths
over the cage,

for permafrost, lichen crusts
nuzzled by reindeer,
the tender balance of decades
null as a vault.

For all frozen things –
the princess and princes
staring out of their bunker
at the original wind,

for NATO survivors in nuclear moonsuits
whirled from continent to continent

like Okies in bumpy Fords
fleeing the dustbowl.

For all frozen things –
snowdrops and Christmas roses
blasted down to the germ
of their genetic zip-code.

They fly by memory –
cargo of endless winter,
clods of celeriac, chipped
turnips, lanterns at ten a.m.

in the gloom of a Finnish market-place;
flowers under glass, herring,
little wizened apples.

For all frozen things –
the nipped fish in a mess of ice,
the uncovered galleon
tossed from four centuries of memory,

for nuclear snowsuits bouncing on dust,
trapped on the rough ride of the earth's surface,
on the rough swing of its axis,

like moon-men lost on the moon
watching the earth's green flush

tremble and perish.

Anna Akhmatova

'DISTANCE COLLAPSED IN RUBBLE'

Distance collapsed in rubble and time was shaken,
the devil of speed stamped on the brows
of great mountains and reversed the river's flow,
the seed lay poisoned in the earth,
the sap flowed poisoned in the stem.
A mighty generation of people died out
but everyone knew that the time was very near.

Translated by Richard McKane

Seamus Heaney

AUGURY

The fish faced into the current,
Its mouth agape,
Its whole head opened like a valve.
You said 'It's diseased.'

A pale crusted sore
Turned like a coin
And wound to the bottom,
Unsettling silt off a weed.

We hang charmed
On the trembling catwalk:
What can fend us now
Can soothe the hurt eye

Of the sun,
Unpoison great lakes,
Turn back
The rat on the road.

Alden Nowlan

ST JOHN RIVER

The colour of a bayonet this river
that glitters blue and solid on the page
in tourist folders, yet some thirty towns
use it as a latrine, the sewerage
seeping back to their wells, and farmers maddened
by debt or queer religions winter down
under the ice, the river bottom strewn
with heaps of decomposing bark torn loose
from pulpwood driven south, its acid juice
killing the salmon. August, when the stink
of the corrupted water floats like gas
along these streets, what most astonishes
is that the pictures haven't lied, the real
river is beautiful, as blue as steel.

Michael Hamburger

A DREAM OF WATER

Glimpsed from the wrong side of a motorway,
Still it was light's best mirror,
Its gleam so startling there
That suddenly to swim came back to me,
Thirst of skin, muscle, nerve for a renewal granted
Wherever to immersion it lay open,
Saline or fresh, in surge, in flow, or quiet,
Even by moonlight, double mirror then,
But to be entered, sensed and penetrated:

Clearest, most alien to warm blood
When snow-fed, from alpine slopes
Or pooled within shallows too fast,
Too rocky for limbs to move;
True to itself peat-coloured in the high moorland
   beck,
As in hollows it had reclaimed,
The black slate quarry fed by Welsh rain,
Warmer and brownish in Cornwall's claypit ponds;

In lakes not human yet, so wide
That islets, the far shores
Allured like water's wilderness, till trodden;
Like the seas' otherness, when they sustained and
   killed us
By what they were, each with its moods and weathers:
Current that almost numbed
When air had felt like summer's to one flown in
From a sub-zero north;
The swell that broke reflection;
Stronger, the Biscay undertow
Defied by half-inch lurches
Not for the sake of water, but of land –
So as to look again at light's best mirror.

To concrete, metal, brick
A mirror still, clogged artery of a city,
Could it be more than memory's element here?
The sunlight seen in it left it a river.

Trapped now in alleys where directions lied,
Zigzagging, looping, circling, always diverted
Round a dead centre, away from the blocked-out
    banks,
I could not reach it. Notices warned
Of penalties for trespass on that in which to drown
Is an archaic mercy. Dry voices jeered:
Who will wash water? With what counter-poisons
The poisoners extract from poisoned earth, air, fire?
Wake up. You're one of them, who will not bathe
Till reason is untangled, the lost ends
Run loose as water at the dream's beginning.

Liz Lochhead

WHAT THE POOL SAID, ON MIDSUMMER'S DAY

I've led you by my garrulous banks, babbling
on and on till – drunk on air
and sure it's only water talking –
you come at last to my silence
Listen, I'm dark
and still and deep enough.
Even this hottest gonging sun
on this longest day
can't white me out.
What are you waiting for?
I lie here, inviting, winking you in.

The woman was easy.
Like to like, I called her, she came.
In no time I had her
out of herself, slipping on my water-stockings,
leaning into, being cupped and clasped
in my green glass bra.

But it's you I want, and you know it, man.
I watch you, stripped, knee-deep
in my shallows, telling yourself
that what makes you gasp
and balls your gut
is not my coldness but your own fear.

– Your reasonable fear,
what's true in me admits it.
(Though deeper, oh
older than any reason.)
Yes, I could
drown you, you
could foul my depths, it's not
unheard of. What's fish
in me could make flesh of you,
my wet weeds against your thigh, it
could turn nasty.
I could have you
gulping fistfuls fighting yourself
back from me.

I get darker and darker, suck harder.
On-the-brink man, you
wish I'd flash and dazzle again.
You'd make a fetish of zazzing dragonflies?
You want I should zip myself up
with the kingfisher's flightpath, be beautiful?
I say no tricks. I say just trust,
I'll soak through your skin and
slake your thirst.

I watch. You clench,
clench and come into me.

Stevie Smith

THE RIVER GOD

I may be smelly and I may be old,
Rough in my pebbles, reedy in my pools,
But where my fish float by I bless their swimming
And I like the people to bathe in me, especially women.
But I can drown the fools
Who bathe too close to the weir, contrary to rules.
And they take a long time drowning
As I throw them up now and then in a spirit of clowning.
Hi yih, yippity-yap, merrily I flow,
O I may be an old foul river but I have plenty of go.
Once there was a lady who was too bold
She bathed in me by the tall black cliff where the water runs
    cold,
So I brought her down here
To be my beautiful dear.
Oh will she stay with me will she stay
This beautiful lady, or will she go away?
She lies in my beautiful deep river bed with many a weed
To hold her, and many a waving reed.
Oh who would guess what a beautiful white face lies there
Waiting for me to smooth and wash away the fear
She looks at me with. Hi yih, do not let her
Go. There is no one on earth who does not forget her
Now. They say I am a foolish old smelly river
But they do not know of my wide original bed
Where the lady waits, with her golden sleepy head.
If she wishes to go I will not forgive her.

U.A. Fanthorpe

RISING DAMP

(for C.A.K and R.K.M.)

'A river can sometimes be diverted, but it is a very hard thing to lose it altogether.'
(J.G. Head: paper read to the Auctioneer's Institute in 1907)

At our feet they lie low,
The little fervent underground
Rivers of London

Effra, Graveney, Falcon, Quaggy,
Wandle, Walbrook, Tyburn, Fleet

Whose names are disfigured,
Frayed, effaced.

These are the Magogs that chewed the clay
To the basin that London nestles in.
These are the currents that chiselled the city,
That washed the clothes and turned the mills,
Where children drank and salmon swam
And wells were holy.

They have gone under.
Boxed, like the magician's assistant.
Buried alive in earth.
Forgotten, like the dead.

They return spectrally after heavy rain,
Confounding suburban gardens. They infiltrate
Chronic bronchitis statistics. A silken
Slur haunts dwellings by shrouded
Watercourses, and is taken
For the footing of the dead.

Being of our world, they will return
(Westbourne, caged at Sloane Square,
Will jack from his box),
Will deluge cellars, detonate manholes,
Plant effluent on our faces,
Sink the city.

Effra, Graveney, Falcon, Quarry,
Wandle, Walbrook, Tyburn, Fleet

It is the other rivers that lie
Lower, that touch us only in dreams
That never surface. We feel their tug
As a dowser's rod bends to the source below

Phlegethon, Acheron, Lethe, Styx.

Ray A. Young Bear

THE REASON WHY I AM AFRAID
EVEN THOUGH I AM A FISHERMAN

Who is there
to witness the ice
as it gradually forms itself
from the cold rock-hard banks
to the middle of the river?
Is the wind chill a factor?
Does the water at some point
negotiate and agree to stop
moving and become frozen?
When you do not know the answers
to these immediately you are afraid,
and to even think in this inquisitive
manner is contrary to the precept
that life is in everything.
Me, I am not a man;
I respect the river
for not knowing its secret,
for answers have nothing
to do with cause and occurrence.
It doesn't matter how early
I wake to see the sun shine
through the ice-hole;
only the ice along
with my foolishness
decides when
to break.

Raymond Carver

THE RIVER

I waded, deepening, into the dark water.
Evening, and the push
and swirl of the river as it closed
around my legs and held on.
Young grilse broke water.
Parr darted one way, smolt another.
Gravel turned under my boots as I edged out.
Watched by the furious eyes of king salmon.
Their immense heads turned slowly,
eyes burning with fury, as they hung
in the deep current.
They were there. I felt them there,
and my skin prickled. But
there was something else.
I braced with the wind on my neck.
Felt the hair rise
as something touched my boot.
Grew afraid at what I couldn't see.
Then of everything that filled my eyes –
that other shore heavy with branches,
the dark lip of the mountain range behind.
And this river that had suddenly
grown black and swift.
I drew breath and cast anyway.
Prayed nothing would strike.

Andrew Young

THE FEAR

How often I turn round
To face the beast that bound by bound
Leaps on me from behind,
Only to see a bough that heaves
With sudden gust of wind
Or blackbird raking withered leaves.

A dog may find me out
Or badger toss a white-lined snout;
And one day as I softly trod
Looking for nothing stranger than
A fox or stoat I met a man
And even that seemed not too odd.

And yet in any place I go
I watch and listen as all creatures do
For what I cannot see or hear,
For something warns me everywhere
That even in my land of birth
I trespass on the earth.

Frances Horovitz

WINTER WOODS

air hangs like metal
two swans shrunken
on yellow water
red berries – omens
we cannot decipher
a green leaf startles
                    like blood
whose bones beneath the tree?

we walk – cracking the silence
the daylight moon stares through branches
leprosy invading iron

our warm blood stills
the sun is livid in exile
we have encroached –
this is not yet our land

Frances Horovitz

WALKING IN AUTUMN

(for Diana Lodge)

We have overshot the wood.
The track has led us beyond trees
to the tarmac edge. Too late now
at dusk to return a different way,
hazarding barbed wire or an unknown bull.
We turn back onto the darkening path.
Pale under-leaves of whitebeam, alder
gleam at our feet like stranded fish
or Hansel's stones.
A wren, unseen, churrs alarm:
each tree drains to blackness.
Halfway now, we know
by the leaning crab-apple;
feet crunching into mud
the hard slippery yellow moons.
We hurry without reason
stumbling over roots and stones.
A night creature lurches, cries out,
crashes through brambles.
Skin shrinks inside our clothes;
almost we run
falling through darkness to the wood's end,
the gate into the sloping field.

Home is lights and woodsmoke, voices –
and, our breath caught, not trembling now,
a strange reluctance to enter within doors.

Stevie Smith

OUT OF TIME

It is a formal and deserted garden
With many a flower bed and winding path.
A cupid stands and draws a bow at venture
Upon a marble bath.

All round his feet the eager ivy grows,
Stretches upon the stone, above the ground,
And in the ivy flowers the busy bee
Makes a melodious sound.

The air is languorous with summer scents
And still it lies upon the garden all
As still and secret as it stayed upon
A funeral.

The sun shines brightly in the upper air
And casts his beams upon the garden grass.
There spilled they lie a carpet of dull gold
Where shadows pass.

The garden gives to these primaeval beams
That strew its floor a plastered yellow tone
As of too mellow sunshine that brings on
A thunder stone.

It is an ominous enchanted garden
That can transmogrify the healthful rays,
Can hold and make them an essential part
Of unquiet days.

Ah me, the unquiet days they tread me down,
The hours and minutes beat upon my head.
I have spent here the time of three men's lives
And am not dead.

Emily Dickinson

'THERE'S A CERTAIN SLANT OF LIGHT'

There's a certain Slant of light,
Winter Afternoons –
That oppresses, like the Heft
Of Cathedral Tunes –

Heavenly Hurt, it gives us –
We can find no scar,
But internal difference,
Where the Meanings, are –

None may teach it – Any –
'Tis the Seal Despair –
An imperial affliction
Sent us of the Air –

When it comes, the Landscape listens –
Shadows – hold their breath –
When it goes, 'tis like the Distance
On the look of Death –

Denise Levertov

OVERHEARD OVER S.E. ASIA

'White phosphorous, white phosphorous,
mechanical snow,
where are you falling?'

'I am falling impartially on roads and roofs,
on bamboo thickets, on people.
My name recalls rich seas on rainy nights,
each drop that hits the surface eliciting
luminous response from a million algae.
My name is a whisper of sequins. Ha!
Each of them is a disk of fire.
I am the snow that burns.
                                        I fall
wherever men send me to fall –
but I prefer flesh, so smooth, so dense:
I decorate it in black, and seek
the bone.'

Antoni Malczewski

OPEN SPACES

The warriors gone, these fields are void and still.
Even regret for heroes cannot fill
The heart's emptiness. And the eye loiters here,
Restlessly finding nothing really clear,
'No movement and no calm. The sun slants down.
A black crow and its shadow sometimes clown.
They croak. A cricket chirrups from a clump
Of nearby grass. The air appears to slump.
And why does nothing from the past descend
Gently, ancestrally, now? no august blend
Of grief and exaltation burden us?
Descend indeed, by paths laborious

Beneath the earth to reach a skeleton
Dressed in the armour of some knight unknown.
There, with the rust and ashes, corpses rot,
Warm flesh where worms are hatching. Here, man's thought
Without an aim or limit, like Despair,
Strays over fields, unsheltered by the air.

W.S. Rendra

TWILIGHT VIEW

The wet twilight calms the burning forest.
Vampire bats descend from the dark grey sky.
Smell of munitions in the air. Smell of corpses. And
        horseshit.
A pack of wild dogs
eat hundreds and thousands of human bodies
the dead and the half dead.
And among the scorched trees of the forest
puddles of blood form into a pool.
Wide and calm. Ginger in colour.
Twenty angels come down from heaven
to purify those in their death throes
but on earth are ambushed by the giant vampires
and raped.
A vital breeze which travels gently on
moves away the ringlet curls of the corpses
makes circles on the lake of blood
and impassions the lust of angels and bats.
Yes, my brothers.
I know this is a view which satisfies you
for you have worked so intently to create it.

Translated by Harry Aveling

David Jones

From IN PARENTHESIS

The gentle slopes are green to remind you
of South English places, only far wider and flatter spread and
grooved and harrowed criss-cross whitely and the disturbed
subsoil heaped up albescent.

Across upon this undulated board of verdure chequered
bright
when you look to left and right
small, drab, bundled pawns severally make effort
moved in tenuous line
and if you looked behind – the next wave came slowly, as suc-
cessive surfs creep in to dissipate on flat shore;
and to your front, stretched long laterally,
and receded deeply,
the dark wood.

And now the gradient runs more flatly toward the separate
scared saplings, where they make fringe for the interior thicket
and you take notice.
    There between the thinning uprights
at the margin
straggle tangled oak and flayed sheeny beech-bole, and fragile
birch whose silver queenery is draggled and ungraced
and June shoots lopt
and fresh stalks bled
            runs the Jerry trench.
And cork-screw stapled trip-wire
to snare among the briars
and iron warp with bramble weft
with meadow-sweet and lady-smock
for a fair camouflage.

Ruth Fainlight

THE FIELD

The field is trampled over utterly.
No hidden corner remains unchurned.
Unusable henceforth for pasture:
Sheep and cattle must feed elsewhere.

The field was torn by battle, dull
Explosions, trenches dug for shelter,
Vehicles which wheeled, reversed,
Hunted down the last resistance.

The field is strewn with bones and metal.
Earth which had not felt the air
During millennia, is now revealed
To every element and influence.

The undersoil surprises by its richness.
In battle's lull, at night, the farmer crawls
To estimate what might be salvaged
Of his lone field's potentiality.

If he survives, the field holds promise
Of great abundance, a yield astonishing,
Unprecedented as all he hopes for.
The field is fertile. He must survive.

Mahmud Darwish

WE ARE ENTITLED TO LOVE AUTUMN

We are entitled to love the end of this autumn and ask:
Is there room for another autumn in the field to rest our bodies like
 coal?
An autumn lowering its leaves like gold. I wish we were fig leaves
 I wish we were an abandoned plant
To witness the change of the seasons. I wish we didn't say goodbye
 to the south of the eye so as to ask what
Our fathers had asked when they flew on the tip of the spear. Poetry
 and God's name will be merciful to us.
We are entitled to dry the nights of lovely women, and talk
 about what
Shortens the night for two strangers waiting for the north to reach the
 compass.
An autumn. Indeed we are entitled to smell the scent of this autumn,
 to ask the night for a dream.
Does a dream fall sick like the dreamers? An autumn, an autumn.
 Can a people be born on the guillotine?
We are entitled to die the way we want to die. Let the land hide in an
 ear of wheat.

Antonio Machado

TODAY'S MEDITATION

The fiery palm tree in front of me,
that the setting sun is just now leaving,
this late and silent afternoon,
inside our peaceful garden,
while flowery old Valencia
drinks the Guadalaviar waters –
Valencia of delicate towers,
in the joyful sky of Ausias March,
her river turns entirely into roses
before it arrives at the sea –
I think of the war. The war
is like a tornado moving
through the bleak foothills of the Duero,
through the plains of standing wheat,
from the farmlands of Extremadura
to these gardens with private lemons,
from the grey skies of the north
to these salty marshes full of light.
I think of Spain, all of it sold out,
river by river, mountain by mountain, sea to sea.

Translated by Robert Bly

Hugh MacDiarmid

ONE OF THESE DAYS

The very sea will turn against you.
It will rear itself into a mighty wave
And come roaring like a thousand storms
Gathering speed across the bay
Crashing over the cliffs and over the land
Carrying your homesteads with it,
Your ricks, your boats, your cattle, your children
Engulfing them, choking them in its green belly,
Tossing them abroad like straws,
Casting their pitiful corpses
High up upon the inland moors,
Wasting its roaring power among the rocks,
Laying siege to the everlasting summits,
Then sinking back to the ocean bed
Leaving a featureless land behind,
Stript naked of every sign of human life,
Nothing but a vast mudbank
And a heavy savour of salt . . .
In the meantime it flickers below you
Like a little methylated spirits
Set alight in a bowl.

Lavinia Greenlaw

THE RECITAL OF LOST CITIES

It started with the polar ice caps.
A slight increase in temperature and the quiet
was shattered. The Australian Antarctic
wandered all over the Norwegian Dependency
as mountainous fragments lurched free
with a groan like ship's mahogany.

And then there was the continental shift:
everywhere you went, America was coming closer.
Hot weather brought plague and revolution.
Nations disappeared or renamed themselves
as borders moved in, out, in, out,
reminiscent of the long gone tide.

Cartographers dealt in picture postcards.
The printing plates for the last atlas
were archived unused. Their irrelevant contours
gathered dust, locked in a vault
to save the public from the past
and the danger of wrong directions.

The sea rose by inches, unravelled the coastline,
eased across the lowlands and licked at the hills
where people gathered to remember names:
Calcutta, Tokyo, San Francisco,
Amsterdam, Baku, Alexandria,
Venice, Norwich, Santo Domingo . . .

Charlotte Mew

DOMUS CAEDET ARBOREM

Ever since the great planes were murdered at the end of the gardens
    The city, to me, at night has the look of a Spirit brooding crime;
As if the dark houses watching the trees from dark windows
    Were simply biding their time.

James Thomson

From THE CITY OF DREADFUL NIGHT

The City is of Night; perchance of Death,
  But certainly of Night; for never there
Can come the lucid morning's fragrant breath
  After the dewy dawning's cold grey air;
The moon and stars may shine with scorn or pity;
The sun has never visited that city,
  For it dissolveth in the daylight fair.

★ ★ ★

A river girds the city west and south,
  The main north channel of a broad lagoon,
Regurging with the salt tides from the mouth;
  Waste marshes shine and glister to the moon
For leagues, then moorland black, then stony ridges;
Great piers and causeways, many noble bridges,
  Connect the town and islet suburbs strewn.

Upon an easy slope it lies at large,
  And scarcely overlaps the long curved crest
Which swells out two leagues from the river marge.
  A trackless wilderness rolls north and west,
Savannahs, savage woods, enormous mountains,
Bleak uplands, black ravines with torrent fountains;
  And eastward rolls the shipless sea's unrest.

The city is not ruinous, although
  Great ruins of an unremembered past,
With others of a few short years ago
  More sad, are found within its precincts vast.
The street-lamps always burn; but scarce a casement
In house or palace front from roof to basement
  Doth glow or gleam athwart the mirk air cast.

The street-lamps burn amidst the baleful glooms,
    Amidst the soundless solitudes immense
Of rangèd mansions dark and still as tombs.
    The silence which benumbs or strains the sense
Fulfils with awe the soul's despair unweeping:
Myriads of habitants are ever sleeping,
    Or dead, or fled from nameless pestilence!

Alfonsina Storni

MEN IN THE CITY

The forests of the
horizon burn;
dodging flames,
the blue bucks
of the twilight
cross quickly.

Little gold goats
emigrate toward
the arch of the sky
and lie down
on blue moss.

Below,
there rises,
enormous,
the cement rose,
the city
unmoving on its stem
of somber basements.

Its black pistils –
dormers, towers –
emerge
to wait for lunar
pollen.

Suffocated
by the flames of bonfires,
and lost
among the petals
of the rose,
almost invisible,
moving from one side toward the other,
the men . . .

Translated by Marion Freeman

Margaret Atwood

A HOLIDAY

My child in the smoke of the fire
playing at barbarism,
the burst meat dripping down her
chin, soot smearing
her cheek and her hair infested with twigs,
under a huge midsummer-leafed tree
in the rain, the shelter
of poles and canvas down
the road if needed:

This could be where we
end up, learning the minimal
with maybe no tree, no rain,
no shelter, no roast carcasses
of animals to renew us

at a time when language
will shrink to the word *hunger*
and the word *none*.

Mist lifts from the warm lake
hit by the cold drizzle:
too much dust in the stratosphere
this year, they say. Unseasonal.

Issa

'NEVER FORGET'

Never forget:
we walk on hell,
gazing at flowers.

Elaine Feinstein

BY THE CAM

Tonight I think this landscape could
    easily swallow me: I'm smothering
in marshland, wet leaves, brown
    creepers, puddled in
rain and mud, one little gulp and

I'll be gone without a splutter:
    into night, flood, November, rot and
river-scud. Scoopwheeled for drainage.
    And by winter, the fen will be brittle and
pure again, an odd, tough, red leaf frozen
    out of its year into the ice of the gutter.

George Crabbe

From THE POOR OF THE BOROUGH

LETTER XXII, PETER GRIMES

Thus by himself compell'd to live each day,
To wait for certain hours the tide's delay;
At the same times the same dull views to see,
The bounding marsh-bank and the blighted
    tree;
The water only, when the tides were high,
When low, the mud half-cover'd and half-dry;
The sun-burnt tar that blisters on the planks,
And bank-side stakes in their uneven ranks;
Heaps of entangled weeds that slowly float,
As the tide rolls by the impeded boat.
  When tides were neap, and, in the sultry day,
Through the tall bounding mud-banks made
    their way,
Which on each side rose swelling, and below
The dark warm flood ran silently and slow;
There anchoring, Peter chose from man to
    hide,
There hang his head, and view the lazy tide
In its hot slimy channel slowly glide;
Where the small eels that left the deeper way
For the warm shore, within the shallows
    play;
Where gaping muscles, left upon the mud,
Slope their slow passage to the fallen flood;—
Here dull and hopeless he'd lie down and trace
How sidelong crabs had scrawl'd their crooked
    race;
Or sadly listen to the tuneless cry
Of fishing gull or clanging golden-eye;
What time the sea-birds to the marsh would
    come,

And the loud bittern, from the bull-rush
    home,
Gave from the salt-ditch side the bellowing
    boom:
He nursed the feelings these dull scenes
    produce,
And loved to stop beside the opening sluice;
Where the small stream, continued in narrow
    bound,
Ran with a dull, unvaried, sadd'ning sound;
Where all, presented to the eye or ear,
Oppress'd the soul with misery, grief, and fear.

Thomas Hardy

NIGHT-TIME IN MID-FALL

It is a storm-strid night, winds footing swift
    Through the blind profound;
  I know the happenings from their sound;
Leaves totter down still green, and spin and drift;
The tree-trunks rock to their roots, which wrench and lift
The loam where they run onward underground.

The streams are muddy and swollen; eels migrate
    To a new abode;
  Even cross, 'tis said, the turnpike-road;
(Men's feet have felt their crawl, home-coming late):
The westward fronts of towers are saturate,
Church-timbers crack, and witches ride abroad.

John Milton

From PARADISE LOST
BOOK II

Another part, in squadrons and gross bands,
On bold adventure to discover wide
That dismal world, if any clime perhaps
Might yield them easier habitation, bend
Four ways their flying march, along the banks
Of four infernal rivers, that disgorge
Into the burning lake their baleful streams:
Abhorrèd Styx, the flood of deadly hate;
Sad Acheron of sorrow, black and deep;
Cocytus, named of lamentation loud
Heard on the rueful stream; fierce Phlegethon,
Whose waves of torrent fire inflame with rage.
Far off from these, a slow and silent stream,
Lethe, the river of oblivion, rolls
Her watery labyrinth, whereof who drinks
Forthwith his former state and being forgets,
Forgets both joy and grief, pleasure and pain.
Beyond this flood a frozen continent
Lies dark and wild, beat with perpetual storms
Of whirlwind and dire hail, which on firm land
Thaws not, but gathers heap, and ruin seems
Of ancient pile; all else deep snow and ice,
A gulf profound as that Serbonian bog
Betwixt Damiata and Mount Casius old,
Where armies whole have sunk: the parching air
Burns frore, and cold performs the effect of fire.

★   ★   ★

Thus roving on
In confused march forlorn, the adventurous bands,
With shuddering horror pale and eyes aghast,
Viewed first their lamentable lot, and found
No rest. Through many a dark and dreary vale
They passed, and many a region dolorous,
O'er many a frozen, many a fiery Alp,
Rocks, caves, lakes, fens, bogs, dens, and shades of
    death –
A universe of death, which God by curse
Created evil, for evil only good;
Where all life dies, death lives, and Nature breeds,
Perverse, all monstrous, all prodigious things,
Abominable, unutterable, and worse
Than fables yet have feigned or fear conceived,
Gorgons, and Hydras, and Chimaeras dire.

James Thomson

From THE SEASONS

SUMMER

'Tis raging noon; and, vertical, the sun
Darts on the head direct his forceful rays.
O'er heaven and earth, far as the ranging eye
Can sweep, a dazzling deluge reigns; and all
From pole to pole is undistinguish'd blaze.
In vain the sight, dejected, to the ground
Stoops for relief; thence hot-ascending steams
And keen reflection pain. Deep to the root
Of vegetation parch'd, the cleaving fields
And slippery lawn an arid hue disclose,
Blast Fancy's bloom, and wither e'en the soul.
Echo no more returns the cheeful sound
Of sharpening scythe: the mower sinking heaps
O'er him the humid hay, with flowers perfumed;
And scarce a chirping grasshopper is heard
Through the dumb mead. Distressful Nature pants.
The very streams look languid from afar;
Or, through the unshelter'd glade, impatient, seem
To hurl into the covert of the grove.

Kwesi Brew

THE DRY SEASON

The year is withering; the wind
Blows down the leaves;
Men stand under eaves
And overhear the secrets
Of the cold dry wind,
Of the half-bare trees.

The grasses are tall and tinted,
Straw-gold hues of dryness,
And the contradicting awryness,
Of the dusty roads a-scatter
With pools of colourful leaves,
With ghosts of the dreaming year.

And soon, soon the fires,
The fires will begin to burn,
The hawk will flutter and turn
On its wings and swoop for the mouse,
The dogs will run for the hare,
The hare for its little life.

Robert Penn Warren

SUMMER STORM (CIRCA 1916), AND GOD'S GRACE

Toward sun, the sun flared suddenly red.
    The green of woods was doused to black.
    The cattle bellowed by the haystack.
Redder than ever, red clay was red.
    Up the lane the plowhands came pelting back.

Astride and no saddle, and they didn't care
    If a razor-back mule at a break-tooth trot
    Was not the best comfort a man ever got,
But came huddling on, with jangling gear,
    And the hat that jounced off stayed off, like as not.

In that strange light all distance died.
    You know the world's intensity.
    Field-far, you can read the aphid's eye.
The mole, in his sod, can no more hide,
    And weeps beneath the naked sky.

Past silence, sound insinuates
    Past ear into the inner brain.
    The toad's asthmatic breath is pain,
The cutworm's tooth grinds and grates,
    And the root, in earth, screams, screams again,

But no cloud yet. No wind, though you,
    A half a county off, now spy
    The crow that, laboring zenith-high,
Is suddenly, with wings askew,
    Snatched, and tumbled down the sky.

And so you wait. You cannot talk.
    The creek-side willows shudder gray.
    The oak leaves turn the other way,
Gray as fish-belly. Then, with a squawk,
    The henhouse heaves, and flies away,

And darkness rides in on the wind.
    The pitchfork lightning tosses the trees,
    And God gets down on hands and knees
To peer and cackle and commend
    His own sadistic idiocies.

Next morning you stood where the bridge had washed out.
    A drowned cow bobbled down the creek.
    Raw-eyed, men watched. They did not speak.
Till one shrugged, said he guessed he'd make out.
    Then turned, took the woods-path up the creek.

King James Bible

JEREMIAH 4

    I beheld the earth, and, lo, it was waste
and void; and the heavens, and they had no
light.
    I beheld the mountains, and, lo, they
trembled, and all the hills moved to and fro.

I beheld, and, lo, thre was no man, and all
the birds of the heavens were fled.

I beheld, and, lo, the fruitful field was a
wilderness, and all the cities thereof were
broken down at the presence of the Lord,
and before his fierce anger.

For thus saith the Lord, The whole land
shall be a desolation; yet will I not make a
full end.

For this shall the earth mourn, and the
heavens above be black: because I have
spoken it, I have purposed it, and I have not
repented, neither will I turn back from it.

Nina Cassian

AND WHEN SUMMER COMES TO AN END . . .

And when summer comes to an end
it's like the world coming to an end.
Wilderness and terror – everywhere!

Days shrink
till all dignity's gone.
Wet slabs of cloth
drape our bodies:
dejected coats.
And then we shiver, stumbling
into the holes of Winter Street
on the corner of Decline. . .

What's the good of living
with the idea of Spring
– dangerous as any Utopia?

Biographical Notes

Anna Akhmatova (1889–1966) USSR
Spent most of her life in St Petersburg (later Leningrad) and suffered much under
Stalin; her son was imprisoned for a long period and, in 1946, she was denounced
and expelled from the Writers Union (Zhdanov attacked her as a 'half nun, half
whore'). She was rehabilitated under Khrushchev and by the time of her death was
widely recognised as a great poet.

Ahmad 'Abd al–Mu'ti Hijází (1935–) Egypt
Hijází was born in a village in the Nile Delta in 1935 and he studied at the
Teachers' College in Cairo. He has published *Madínah bilá Qalb* (City Without a
Heart), *Lam Yabqa illá al-I'tiráf* (Nothing Remains but Confession) and *Urás* (Horace).

Abd Allah ibn al–Simak (d.1145) Spain

Paula Gunn Allen (1939–) USA
Poet, novelist and critic. Born in Cubero, Mexico, of Laguna, Sioux and Lebanese
origin, her poetry collections include *The Blind Lion* (1974), *Coyotes Daylight Trip*
(1978), *A Cannon Between My Knees* (1981). She has also written a novel, *The
Woman Who Owned the Shadows* (1983), and edited the collection, *Spider Woman's
Granddaughters* (1989).

Gillian Allnutt (1949–) England
Born in London and now lives in Newcastle. A former poetry editor of the London
magazine *City Limits*, she now teaches creative writing. Her collections include
Spitting the Pips out (1981), and *Beginning the Avocado* (1987); she has also written
Berthing: A Poetry Workbook for Women (1991).

Jorge Carrera Andrade (1903–) Ecuador
The son of a liberal lawyer, he became General Secretary of the newly formed
Socialist Party after graduating from Quito University and became an outspoken
supporter of Indian rights in his country. He later held diplomatic postings in coun-
tries including Peru, Venezuela, the Netherlands and the USA.

Anyte (c.290 BC) Greece
Arcadian poet from Tegea who was much admired during her lifetime and remem-
bered by later critics as one of the first poets to write descriptions of the wilderness.
A number of her four-line epigrams have survived, mainly through the *Greek
Anthology*; the compiler of the volume, Meleagros, refers to 'the many lilies of
Anyte' in his preamble. However, the lyrics she is known to have composed are lost.

Margaret Atwood (1939–) Canada
A prolific poet with more than 20 volumes in print, although more often known for her best-selling novels, including *Surfacing* (1972), *The Handmaid's Tale* (1985) and *Cat's Eye* (1989). She is also prominent in contemporary Canadian debates on nationalism and feminism. She was born in Ottawa and grew up in the bush country of Quebec and Ontario.

George Awoonor-Williams (**Kofi Awoonor**) (1935–) Ghana
Poet, novelist, dramatist and critic. He studied and later taught at the University of Ghana. He has been managing director of the Ghana Film Corporation, founder of the Ghana Playhouse and editor of *Okyeame*, a literary review devoted to the publication of traditional African poetry. He writes mainly in English but his work is strongly influenced by his native Ewe culture.

William Barnes (1801–1886) England
Poet, linguist and philologist. He grew up in a Dorset family and then became a local schoolmaster. In 1848 he was ordained as a rector after 10 years of part-time study at Cambridge. He wrote most of his verse in Dorset dialect and was also fluent in Welsh, Hebrew and Hindustani, amongst other languages; contemporary admirers included the poets Thomas Hardy and Alfred Tennyson.

Basho (1644–1694) Japan
Spent his youth as a companion to the son of a local lord and with him studied *haiku*, the strictly 17-syllable verse form. He moved to Edo (now Tokyo) in 1667 where he became a hermit living on the edge of the city and attracting disciples. He spent much of his later life travelling in Japan, relying on the hospitality of temples and fellow poets, and wrote over 1,000 *haiku* and travel sketches. His work was greatly influenced by Zen Buddhism.

Susan Bassnett (1948–) England
Head of Comparative Literature at the University of Warwick, her latest translation is of the Mexican novelist Margot Glantz's *The Family Tree* (Serpent's Tail, 1991). Her translation of Elizabeth Weston's collection *Parthenicon* is to be published in the USA by the Library of Renaissance Humanism.

Frances Bellerby (1899–1975) England
Grew up in a working-class parish of Bristol, where her father was a curate and her mother a nurse. Later she moved to Cornwall and then Devon after working as a drama critic in London. A spinal injury left her a semi-invalid from the age of 31. She wrote one novel and a number of short stories as well as six volumes of poetry.

Marion Bernstein (fl. 1876) Scotland
Little is known in detail about her life. In the preface to *Mirren's Musings, A Collection of Songs and Poems* (1876), written at an address in the Paisley Road, she refers to 'a long period of physical affliction' but reassures concerned friends that she

had since been able to resume her former occupation as a music teacher. She also wrote regularly for the *Glasgow Weekly Mail*. The poem included here (and the one by Patrick Magill) can be found in the excellent anthology *Radical Renfrew* (Polygon, 1990).

Wendell Berry (1934–) USA
Organic farmer and poet who, with the exception of brief periods of study and university teaching, has always lived close to his birthplace near the Kentucky River. He bought part of the land he works in order to save it from ecological disaster but believes that land should only be held in trust by humans, not owned. Much of his poetry charts the adverse effects of agribusiness on the Kentucky region. He is author of numerous books, among them *The Unsettling of America* (1977) and *Home Economics* (1987).

Mary Ursula Bethell (1874–1945) New Zealand
Educated in Europe, she did social work in London before returning to New Zealand during the 1920s. There she established a garden and, at the age of 50, began to write poetry. Her first collection, *From A Garden in the Antipodes* (1929) was published in London under a pseudonym; however she soon became well-known in her own name in New Zealand, playing a central part in Christchurch cultural life during the 1930s and early 1940s.

Elizabeth Bishop (1911–1979) USA
Began publishing poetry while at school in Nova Scotia and Boston, later attending Vassar College, New York, with fellow student and poet, Marianne Moore. She travelled widely before finally settling in Brazil. Collections include *North and South* (1946), *Questions of Travel* (1965) and *Geography III* (1976).

Robert Bly (1926–) USA
'I earn my living giving readings at American colleges and universities, and translating,' he writes. Founder-editor of *The Sixties* magazine and press which aimed to bring South American and European poetry to US audiences. He was active in the US anti-war movement. His translations of Pablo Neruda helped bring the Chilean poet to international fame. Most recently, he is author of the bestselling book *Iron John: A Book About Man*.

Kwesi Brew (1928–) Ghana
One of the first students to graduate from the University College of the Gold Coast (now the University of Ghana), he then worked in various civil service posts before being posted abroad as a diplomat attached to missions as far afield as the Soviet Union and Mexico. His poetry was published in the first issue of the Ghanaian literary review *Okyeame*.

Charlotte Brontë (1816–1855) England
While her novels, in particular *Jane Eyre* (1847), were the subject of critical acclaim

as well as controversy during her lifetime, her poetry received little attention. She lived mainly at her father's vicarage on the Yorkshire Moors, but worked briefly as a governess and spent two years in Brussels teaching and learning languages. She died soon after her marriage to the local curate, probably of an illness connected with pregnancy.

Olga Broumas (1949–) USA
Born in Greece, she lived in the USA as an adolescent for two years and later as a resident college student, before deciding to emigrate. She now works as a fine arts teacher, musician and bodywork therapist, as well as a poet and translator. Collections include *Caritas* (1976), *Beginning with O* (1977) and *What I Love: Selected Translations of Odysseus Elytis* (1986).

George Gordon Byron (1788–1824) England
One of the great Romantic poets, perhaps as well-known for his lifestyle and passionate affairs as for his poetry. The first two cantos of *Childe Harold's Pilgrimage* were published in March 1812, when he 'awoke one morning and found himself famous'.

Ernesto Cardenal (1925–) Nicaragua
Poet, priest and revolutionary. He established a church and commune on a group of islands on Lake Nicaragua, preaching liberation theology and maintaining strong links with the Sandinista guerrillas; the community was ordered to be destroyed in 1977 and he was forced into exile until the overthrow of the Somoza regime. He became Minister of Culture under the subsequent FSLN government. Translated works include *Apocalypse and Other Poems* (1977) and *Zero Hour and Other Documentary Poems* (1979).

Elizabeth Carter (1717–1806) England
As a child she studied Latin, Greek and Hebrew with her brothers and later learnt six other languages including Arabic and Portuguese; her poor health was reportedly the result of too much study. She wrote three volumes of poetry including *Poems on Particular Occasions* (1738); her translation of the Roman writer Epictetus brought her fame across Europe. She was a member of the Bluestocking circle in London and an associate of Dr Johnson.

Raymond Carver (1939–1988) USA
Author of three volumes of short stories and five collections of poetry, he was born in Oregon. The publication of *In A Marine Light* (1987) marked the first time a selection of his work appeared outside the USA. At the time of his death he was acclaimed as one of the most important writers in the United States.

Nina Cassian (1924–) Romania
Well-known poet and composer, her collection *Lady of Miracles* was translated and published in the USA in 1982. Her collection *Call Yourself Alive? Love Poems of*

Nina Cassian (trans. Andrea Deletant and Brenda Walker) was published in the UK in 1988 by Forest Books.

C.P. Cavafy (1863–1933) Egypt
'A Greek gentleman in a straw hat, standing absolutely motionless at a slight angle to the universe' (E.M. Forster). Of Greek parentage, he lived most of his life in Alexandria, where he worked for many years as a clerk in the Ministry of Public Works. His poetry received recognition outside the Greek-speaking world through the influence of E.M. Forster, and was first translated into English in 1951.

Geoffrey Chaucer (c. 1343–1400) England
Poet, translator and civil servant. He wrote the famous *Canterbury Tales* as well as many shorter lyric poems towards the end of his life; his earlier works were heavily influenced by French and Italian literature. Through his marriage he enjoyed the patronage of John of Gaunt.

Amy Clampitt (1920–) USA
Born in Iowa, she now lives in New York, after making her career in publishing and freelance writing. Collections include *The Kingfisher* (1984), *A Homage to John Keats* (1984) and *What the Light was Like* (1985). Her poetry is often compared with that of Hopkins.

John Clare (1793–1864) England
The son of a semi-literate farmhand, he worked as a casual labourer from the beginning of his teens. His poems of rural life initially achieved some success, but then faded into obscurity as the vogue for such verse passed. Spent the last 23 years of his life in an asylum. Interest in his poetry was revived this century, with the appearance of new editions of his works.

John Pepper Clark (1935–) Nigeria
Poet and playwright. Born in the Ijo region of the Niger delta, educated at Ibadan University and then at Princeton (where he wrote his caustic memoir *America, Their America* in 1964. In Nigeria he worked as a civil servant and journalist before becoming Professor of English at the University of Lagos. He has researched Ijo myths and legends and translated the Ijo epic, *The Ozidi Saga* (1966).

Gillian Clarke (1937–) Wales
'Public performance of my own and other people's poetry and teaching creative writing in various ways are my main occupations,' she says. She also works as a part-time lecturer and edits the *Anglo-Welsh Review*. Poetry collections include *Snow on the Mountains* (1971), *The Sundial* (1978), *Letter from a Far Country* (1982) and *Selected Poems* (1985). She is originally from Cardiff and has lived in South Wales for most of her life.

Elizabeth Coatsworth (1893–?) USA
Born in Buffalo, New York. Her poetry includes *Fox Footprints* (1923), *Atlas and*

Beyond (1924), *Compass and Rose* (1929), *The Creaking Stairs* (1949) and *Down Half the World* (1968). She is also known for her children's books and for her novels, which are mostly set in rural New England where she lived, in her own words, 'on a farm overlooking Maine Lake at the end of a country road'.

Charles Cotton (1630–1687) England
First became known as a writer through his burlesque of Virgil, *Scarronides*(1664), which Samuel Pepys praised. However, it was his landscape poetry, *The Wonders of the Peake* (1681) and *Poems on Several Occasions* (1689), later much admired by the poets Wordsworth and Coleridge, which kept his reputation alive until the appearance of a collection edited by J. Buxton in 1958.

Abraham Cowley (1618–1667) England
Erudite scholar known for introducing the irregular (Pindaric) ode into English verse; he wrote metaphysical, epic and satirical poetry as well as pastoral drama, Latin comedy and some prose works. He was educated at Cambridge, but moved to Oxford on the outbreak of the Civil War and later served as a secretary in the Royalist court in exile. On his return to England he was imprisoned briefly as a spy by Cromwell.

William Cowper (1731–1800) England
While training as a lawyer he suffered a breakdown, leading to the first of his attempted suicides and a spell in an asylum; he remained thereafter subject to acute bouts of depression. 'The conviction of sin and expectation of instant judgement never left me', he wrote in his memoirs.

George Crabbe (1754–1832) England
The son of a Suffolk salt-tax collector, he moved to London where he hoped to find fame as a writer; there he was befriended by the philosopher Edmund Burke, who rescued him from destitution and encouraged him to enter the ministry, return to the countryside and write. Poetry includes *The Village* (1783), *The Borough* (1810) and *Tales in Verse* (1812). Byron called him 'Nature's sternest painter yet the best'.

Martyn Crucefix (1956–) England
Born in Trowbridge, Wiltshire, he studied English at Lancaster University and then completed his doctoral thesis on Shelley at Oxford. He now works as a teacher in north London and runs writers' workshops. His poems have appeared in various reviews and magazines, including *The London Review of Books*, the *Times Literary Supplement* and *Ambit*. His collection *Beneath Tremendous Rain* was published in 1990.

Samuel Taylor Coleridge (1772–1834) England
Poet, critic, philospher of the Romantic movement and, for many years, an opium addict. He supported French revolutionary politics while still a classics student at

Cambridge University and planned to set up a commune in New England. As he grew older, however, he turned increasingly to Christianity, an influence which can be seen in many of his later works.

Mahmud Darwish (1941–) Palestine/Lebanon
Born in Lebanon, in 1948 his village was destroyed by the Israelis and he and his family fled to Lebanon. His first collection of poetry appeared in 1960. He was awarded the Lotus Prize by the Union of African-Asian Writers, and since 1971 he has lived in Beirut, where he has been a major figure in the PLO. His collections include *Music of Human Flesh* (1980), and he is one of four poets in *Victims of a Map* (Al Saqi).

J. Kitchener Davies (1902–1952) Wales
Dramatist and poet who wrote in Welsh. He is best known for his verse-drama *Meini Gwegedd*, which was compared to, and many felt was superior to, Dylan Thomas' *Under Milk Wood*.

W.H. Davies (1871–1940) England
Self-educated, he wrote of his experiences as a tramp in England and the USA in *Autobiography of a Super-Tramp* (1908). It was through the encouragement of George Bernard Shaw that he became a writer. His *Complete Poems* appeared in 1963.

Thadious M. Davis (1944–) USA
Editor of a number of anthologies of Black American writers, including *Afro-American Poets since 1955*. She is author of the critical study, *Faulkner's 'Negro': Art and the Southern Context* (1983). Her poetry has appeared in many magazines and anthologies.

Emily Dickinson (1830–1880) USA
Author of more than 1,700 poems, of which only a handful were published in her lifetime. She lived in near-seclusion at her father's house in Amherst, Massachusetts, throughout her life, writing in secret. Her sister discovered her work soon after her death and was responsible for bringing it to public attention.

Rosemary Dobson (1920–) Australia
Born in Sydney, she later studied at Sydney University, but wrote, designed and printed her first poetry collection *Poems* (1937), while still at school. Later works include *Child with a Cockatoo* (1955) and *Cockcrow: Poems* (1965) as well as *Selected Poems* (1973; 1980). She also translates contemporary Russian poetry.

Douris (c.340–c.260BC) Greece
Ruler of Samos, historian, critic and a pupil of Theophrastus. He wrote at least 23 books including a chronicle of the island of Samos, which is ruled, and a history of the Greeks from 370–280 BC.

Michael Drayton (1563–1631) England
Prolific poet who wrote much historical and religious verse as well as odes, satires and sonnets together with the lengthy topographical poem, *Poly-Olbion* (1594). He worked as a page and fell in love with his rich employer's daughter, continuing to adore her until long after she was married. He died in relative poverty but was buried in Westminster Abbey.

William Drummond (1585–1649) Scotland
Became laird of Hawthornden upon the death of his father and turned to writing after a youth spent studying law and learning languages in Europe. Works include hymns, a history of Scotland, a prose meditation on death, *In a Cypresse Grove* (1623) and several poetry collections. He was known amongst his comtemporaries as 'The Scottish Petrarch' for the sonnets he wrote.

John Dryden (1631–1700) England
Poet, dramatist, critic and translator, he was one of the great literary figures of his age. His translations of Juvenal were published in 1692, of Virgil in 1697.

dsh (Dom Sylvester Houedard) (1924–) England
Born on the island of Guernsey, he attended Oxford University before going to St Anselmo College in Rome. He joined the Benedictine Order at Prinknash Abbey in Gloucestershire, and became one of the leading exponents of concrete and visual poetry.

Helen Dunmore (1952–) England
A nursery teacher whose recent collection, *Raw Garden* (1988), explores the impact of centuries of human intervention on the landscape. 'As I grew up,' she says, 'I realised that even such apparently wild places as moors and commons were the product of human decisions and work.'

Ralph Waldo Emerson (1803–1882) USA
Boston-born poet, philosopher and lecturer who was revered in his lifetime as a sage. He developed the quasi-religious concept of Transcendentalism, with its mystic idealism and worship of nature. 'Nature is the incarnation of thought. The world is the mind precipitated', he wrote in his famous essay, *Nature* (1836). Walt Whitman greatly admired his work.

Hans Magnus Enzensberger (1929–) Germany
Born in Bavaria, he spent most of his childhood in Nürnberg and then lived in the USA, Mexico, Cuba, Italy and Norway before returning to Germany to settle in Munich. After working as a radio producer in the late 1950s, he turned to freelance writing, becoming a well-known editor, critic, translator and anthologist as well as poet. His *Selected Poems* (1968) were first translated into English by Michael Hamburger.

Ruth Fainlight (1931 –) USA/England
Her childhood was divided between her birthplace, New York City, and England, where she attended both Birmingham and Brighton colleges of art. She then lived in France, Spain and Morocco before settling in London, and has published more than 14 volumes of poetry as well as short stories and translations from Portuguese, Catalan and Spanish.

U.A. Fanthorpe (1929–) England
Worked as Head of English at a girls' boarding school for many years before leaving to do various temporary jobs, eventually becoming a hospital clerk in Bristol between 1974 and 1983. She now lives in Gloucestershire. Her poetry includes *Side Effects* (1978), *Standing To* (1982) and *Voices Off* (1984) as well as *Selected Poems* (1986).

Elaine Feinstein (1930–) England
Grew up in Leicester before studying at Cambridge University, later teaching undergraduates there as well as working on the editorial staff of the Cambridge University Press. She has translated Marina Tsvetayeva's poetry from the Russian. Her own poetry includes *The Magic Apple Tree* (1971), *Some Unease and Angels* (1977) and *City Music* (1990). She has also written eight novels and a number of radio plays.

Anne Finch (1661–1720) England
A maid of honour to Mary of Modena, she was also a literary critic, translator and poet; her transgression of traditional women's roles was deemed unacceptable by society and she was satirised in contemporary plays. In her own work she often wrote about women, launched attacks on other many well-known male writers and court life in general. A friend of Pope, Swift and Gay.

Rose Flint (1944–) England
Trained as a sculptor at Hammersmith College of Art in London, and then worked for several years in publishing. After moving to the west of England she co-founded a women's poetry group based in the Welsh borders called 'Out of Bounds'. For two years she was chair of her local green party. Her first collection, *Blue Horse of Morning* (1991) is published by Seren.

Johann Wolfgang von Goethe (1749–1832) Germany
Trained as a lawyer but spent most of his adult life as a courtier to the Duke of Weimar. He was eventually raised to the nobility and became director of the Weimar Court Theatre. Many of his lyric poems were set to music by German Romantic composers. His best-known work outside Germany is the poetic drama *Faust*.

Janice Gould (1949–) USA
Poet and writer from the Maidu tribe. She was born in San Diego and later graduated from the University of California, Berkeley, in linguistics.

W. S. Graham (1918–1986) Scotland
Trained as an engineer after a Clydeside upbringing and later moved to Cornwall, where he lived and worked as a full-time writer of great accomplishment and originality.

Lavinia Greenlaw (1962–) England
Born in London, she worked as an editor in publishing for several years. In 1990 she won an Eric Gregory award, and her work has been widely anthologised. A booklet *The Cost of Getting Lost in Space* (1991) was published by Turret Books, and she is currently finishing her first collection.

Angelina Weld Grimké (1880–1958) USA
Born in Boston, Massachusetts into a privileged background, she was first published in 1893 and was one of the first Black poets to receive general recognition in the USA. She wrote a pioneering protest play, *Rachel*, and her poetry has been included in many anthologies, including *Carolling Dusk* (ed. Cullen, 1927) and *New Negro Renaissance* (eds Peplow and Davis, 1975).

Ivor Gurney (1890–1937) England
Poet and composer. After sustaining serious injuries during World War I (he was gassed in the Somme) he spent the rest of his life in an asylum, where he continued to write poetry, music and songs. He grew up in Gloucestershire and then studied at the Royal College of Music, London, on a scholarship. Poetry includes *Severn and Somme* (1917) and *War's Embers* (1919).

H.D. [Hilda Doolittle] (1886–1961) USA
Poet and novelist from Pennsylvania. She settled in England following her marriage in 1913 and edited the Imagist periodical *The Egoist*. She was in analysis with Freud for many years, writing the prose work *Tribute to Freud* (1956). Poetry collections include *Sea Garden* (1916), *Hymen* (1921), *Collected Poems* (1925; 1940) and *Helen in Egypt* (1961).

Michael Hamburger (1924–) Germany/England
He left Berlin as a boy, together with most of his German Jewish family, soon after the rise of Hitler to power. They settled first in Edinburgh and then later moved to London. He has since held various academic posts, including lecturer in German at the Universities of London and Reading, and is known for his prize-winning translations of German poetry and critical works, as well as his own poetry.

Thomas Hardy (1840–1928) England
Celebrated novelist who always claimed that he wrote fiction only for money and that poetry was his real vocation. He published eight volumes of poetry, from *Wessex Poems* (1898) through to *Winter Words* (1928); none received recognition until long after his death. His verse, like his fiction, is rooted in the Dorset countryside.

Seamus Heaney (1939–) Ireland
One of the best-known contemporary Irish poets, he grew up in County Derry, and studied at Queen's University, Belfast, where he belonged to a circle of younger Irish poets during the 1960s. He lectured in poetry at Queens for six years and then moved south to Dublin where he now lives. His reputation as one of the finest living poets was established outside Ireland through the collection. *Death of a Naturalist* (1966).

Nazim Hikmet (1902–1963) Turkey
As an advocate of international communism in 1938 he was sentenced by military courts to a total of 35 years' imprisonment on charges of incitement. Following his 1950 hunger strike and international protests, he was released during a general amnesty, and left Turkey for the USSR where he lived in Moscow. He was a prolific poet and also wrote a number of plays.

Molly Holden (1927–1981) England
Began writing in the early 1960s, only a few years before the onset of multiple sclerosis, the disease which confined her to a wheelchair and eventually caused her death. Works include *To Make Me Grieve* (1968), *Air and Chill Earth* (1974) and *The Country Over* (1975). Despite the appearance of *New and Selected Poems*, much of her poetry has yet to be published.

Friedrich Hölderlin (1770–1843) Germany
Wrote most of his poetry and hymns in the period before his mental collapse in 1802; however, he recovered sufficiently to do occasional writing and translation work and lived to be 73. He sympathised with the French Revolution as a student and became a friend of the philosophers Hegel and Schelling. He later preferred to work as a private tutor, rather than enter the Church for which he had been trained.

Gerard Manley Hopkins (1844–1889) England
Came from a High Anglican family but converted to Roman Catholicism under the influence of Cardinal Newman while a student at Oxford. Having become a Jesuit priest, he spent four years in Wales as a professor of rhetoric and a student of the Welsh language. Later he held a post at University College, Dublin, where he became ill and sank into depression. He died of typhoid. His poetry was first published 30 years after his death.

Horace (65–8BC) Rome
His father, a freedman, gave him the best education available, sending him to study in Rome and later in Athens. He was stripped of his property after fighting for the losing side (Brutus's Republican Army) at the Battle of Philippi and was forced to write for a living. A patron eventually installed him in a villa near Tivoli. All of his known works, including *Odes, Epistles* and *Satires*, have survived.

Frances Horovitz (1938–1983) England
Actress, broadcaster and poet. She worked as a school teacher as well as in radio and on the stage after training at RADA. Much of her poetry evokes landscapes of Gloucestershire where she lived for some years, as well as of Northumberland where she moved shortly before her early death. Collections include *The High Tower* (1970), *Water Over Stone* (1980) and *Snow Light, Water Light* (1983).

Hsü Ling (507–583) China

Langston Hughes (1902–1967) USA
Novelist, poet, playwright, essayist and short-story writer from Joplin, Missouri. He enrolled in Columbia University but left before graduating to become involved in the Harlem Renaissance, with his early poetry appearing in the Black review, *The Crisis*. He went on to found Black theatre groups in Harlem, Chicago and Los Angeles and to edit collections of Black folklore, poetry and stories.

John Ceiriog Hughes (19th century) Wales

Issa (1763–1827) Japan
The eldest son of a poor farmer, he experienced much hardship as he grew up. He later travelled frequently between Edo (Tokyo) and the mountains of Nagano. He was not famed as a poet during his lifetime but is today ranked with the much admired *haiku* poet, Basho.

Mieczyslaw Jastrun (1903–) Poland
Wrote under the pseudonym Mieczyslaw Agatstein, publishing four volumes of poetry by World War II while employed as a teacher. Under Nazi occupation he worked with the underground resistance, continuing to teach and write even though, since he was Jewish, his life was in constant danger. He also translated the German poet Rilke and wrote one novel, *The Beautiful Sickness* (1961).

David Jones (1895–1974) England
Son of a printer, he studied painting before serving as a private on the Western Front 1915–1918. After the war he returned to painting, and in 1921 he was received into the Catholic Church. *In Parenthesis* (1937) was hailed as 'a work of genius' by T.S. Eliot.

Juvenal (c. AD 55–?) Rome
Native of Aquinius on the Via Latina in Latium, often heralded as the greatest of the Roman poets. Little is known about his life and what does exist is mostly unreliable; however all sources refer to a period of exile after he offended a favourite of the Emperor Domitian and it seems from his satires that he was once poor, but later acquired a farm at Tibur and a house in Rome.

John Keats (1795–1821) England
Leading Romantic poet whose notion of 'negative capability' advocated a constant

readiness to accept and respond to contradictions and diversity. Apprenticed as an apothecary-surgeon but opted instead for the life of a full-time poet, despite the financial insecurity it entailed. Most of his best known works were written in the three years preceding his death, in Rome, of consumption.

Mary Leapor (1722–1746) England
Her father was a gardener on the Northampton estate of a judge, and although she received little education beyond basic literacy she was writing poems at the age of 10. Just before her sudden death from measles her work attracted the attention of a possible patron and the hope of support for her writing. The posthumous collection, *Poems on Several Occasions* (1748), went into several editions.

Joyce Isabel Lee (1913–) Australia
Born in Murtoa, Victoria, she qualified as a pharmacist. She was lecturer in Poetry Writing at Victoria College, Melbourne from 1981 to 1987. Her collections include *Sisters Poets I* (1979) and *Abruptly from the Flatlands* (1984).

Denise Levertov (1923–) USA
Originally from Essex, she worked as a nurse during World War II before emigrating to the USA with her American husband. Became a university lecturer and prominent leftist, active in the women's movement and outspoken in her opposition to war and Western exploitation of the Third World. Publications include *Collected Earlier Poems 1940–60* (1979), *Poems 1960–67* (1983) and *Selected Poems* (1986).

Liz Lochhead (1947–) Scotland
Studied and then taught art in Glasgow before making a living as a poet, dramatist and reviewer. 'I want my poems to be clear. They should make sense to my landlady and the man in the corner shop. But be capable of being pondered over by the academics round at the University, if they like to,' she says. Books include *The Grimm Sisters* (1981) and *Dreaming Frankenstein* (1984).

Maria Logan (fl. 1793) England
Author of *Poems on Several Occasions* (1793), a collection of occasional and epistolary verses published in York in two editions. In the preface she writes of 'seven years of uninterrupted sickness', while one of the poems refers to opium as both a painkiller and a stimulus to poetic inspiration; little else is known about her life. Several critics praised her work although the subscribers to her volume were mainly local.

Pat Lowther (1935–1975) Canada
Murdered at the age of 40, she was co-chair of the League of Canadian Poets at the time of her death. Her fourth poetry collection, *A Stone Dairy* (1977), came out posthumously, and contains a long sequence about the Chilean poet, Pablo Neruda.

Norman MacCaig (1910–) Scotland
Edinburgh poet with more than 20 volumes of poetry to his name, beginning with

Far Cry (1943). He worked as a schoolteacher for many years, then spent a brief period as a headmaster, eventually becoming a lecturer at the University of Stirling. His *Collected Poems* was published in 1990.

Hugh MacDiarmid (1892–1978) Scotland
Poet, critic, writer, translator, editor and political activist. Wrote much of his early poetry in Scottish Gaelic, becoming a leading figure in the renaissance of Scots culture this century. He remained involved in political debate and controversy throughout his life and was expelled from the Scottish Nationalist Party (SNP), which he helped to found, as well as the Communist Party, which he later rejoined.

Antonio Machado (1875–1939) Spain
Grew up in Seville and worked as a teacher of French literature in Castilian schools for much of his life, but spent some time in Paris at the turn of the century (where he studied under the French philosopher Bergson). He became a spokesperson for the Republicans during the Spanish Civil War, addressing social, political and cultural matters of the day through his prose and essays. He died in southern France three weeks after fleeing from Franco's forces in 1939.

Patrick Magill (1891–1963) Ireland/Scotland
Originally from Donegal where he worked as a farmhand from a young age, he travelled to Scotland aged 14 and survived through a variety of means, ranging from tramp to drainer, wrestler and navvy. By his early twenties he had several works in print, including *Soldiers Songs* (1917) and *Songs from the Dead End* (1920). He later moved to London, working for *The Daily Express* from 1911 onwards.

Antoni Malczewski (1793–1826) Poland
Lived a short but adventurous life, serving in the army, travelling abroad and in 1818 conquering Mont Blanc. He was not well-known as a poet during his own lifetime, but shortly after his death the Polish critic and radical philosopher, Maurycy Mochnacki, espoused his writing as a model of Romanticism.

Andrew Marvell (1621–1678) England
Little of his metaphysical poetry was published during his lifetime (he was known rather as a political satirist); however by the 19th century he was celebrated as 'the green poet' for his pastoral poems. After studying at Cambridge, he worked as a tutor for leading Puritans of the day, including Cromwell's ward, and was a friend and assistant to Milton in his post as Latin Secretary. He later became the Member of Parliament for Hull, remaining an outspoken critic of the restored monarchy until his death.

Richard McKane England
Poet and translator, well-known for his translations of Anna Akhmatova, Nazim Hikmet and Osip Mandelstam in particular. He studied Russian at Oxford

University and then lived in Turkey during the 1970s before obtaining a one-year fellowship at Princeton University. His latest translations are in *Poetry* of *Perestroika* (eds McKane & Rumens, 1991).

Claude McKay (1890–1948) USA/Jamaica
Poet and novelist. He emigrated to the USA from Jamaica in 1912, publishing *Songs of Jamaica* later the same year. His work attracted good reviews, but it was not until the publication of *Harlem Shadows* (1922) that he gained wide recognition as a poet. His novels include *Home to Harlem* (1928) and *Banana Bottom* (1933).

Charlotte Mew (1869–1928) England
Born in Bloomsbury, London, the daughter of an architect. She published only two collections, *The Farmer's Bride* (1915) and *The Rambling Sailor* (1929), but many contemporaries, including Thomas Hardy, thought her the best woman poet of her time. She suffered ill-health, poverty and depression, which led to her suicide after her sister's death. Her *Collected Poems and Prose* was published in 1982.

Terri Meyette (c. 1954–) USA
Began writing poetry while serving a prison sentence in Goodyear, Arizona. She is from the Yaqui tribe.

Czeslaw Milosz (1911–) Poland
Born in Lithuania, he was raised in Czarist Russia and became a leading figure in the Polish avant-garde poetry movement during the 1930s. He edited an anti-Nazi anthology as part of the resistance during the Second World War. In 1951 he defected to the West, eventually settling in the USA, where he has taught Slavic languages and literature for many years. He writes in Polish.

John Milton (1608–1674) England
Moved from writing lyric poetry as a student to political pamphleteering as the Latin Secretary to the Commonwealth under Cromwell. Following the restoration of the monarchy he returned to poetry and began composing the epic *Paradise Lost* (1667), his most famous work. He is generally regarded as responsible for popularising the use of blank verse in poetry, until then largely confined to drama.

Rosario Morales, USA
An American born of Puerto Rican parents, she lived in Puerto Rico for eleven years. The landscapes of that mountain home haunt many of her poems and stories.

Les A. Murray (1938–) Australia
Publications include *The Ilex Tree* (1965), *Poems Against Economics* (1972) and *Selected Poems: The Vernacular Republic* (1976) as well as a verse-novel and a collection of essays and reviews. He worked as a translator at the Australian National University, Canberra, for four years and has adapted aboriginal song-cycles into English. He lives in New South Wales and is presently co-editor of the journal *Poetry Australia*.

Tom Murray (c. 1920–) Australia
Born into a semi-nomadic life, he worked on cattle stations in West Queensland for many years and is now settled at Mount Garnet. He has translated many traditional Jirrbal songs.

Pablo Neruda (1904–1973) Chile
Began writing poetry as a student in Santiago and continued while employed as a diplomat in various postings, including Consul General to the Spanish Republic, 1934–1936. He later joined the Chilean Communist Party, was elected a senator and then spent a period in exile for his politics. Once able to return to Chile, he devoted the rest of his life almost entirely to writing; his poetic output was huge, with *The Collected Works* (1962) running to 1,800 pages.

Norman Nicholson (1914–1987) England
Lived throughout his life in Millom, a small mining community on the Cumberland coast. He edited *The Penguin Anthology of Modern Religious Verse* (1942) and soon after published his first volume of poetry, *Five Rivers* (1944). Later works include *Prophesy of the Wind* (1950) and *The Lakes* (1977) as well as several verse plays.

Alden Nowlan (1933–1983) Canada
Moved from his hometown of Windsor, New Brunswick, where he worked as a farm- and mill-hand, to Fredericton where he became a journalist. He began publishing poetry and short stories from the mid-1950s onwards, including *Wind in a Rocky Country* (1960), *Double Exposure* (1978) and *I might not tell every one this* (1982). Writer-in-residence at the University of New Brunswick from 1968, he was one of Canada's finest, and most popular, poets.

Dorothy Parker (1893–1967) USA
New York journalist, short-story writer and poet, known for her urbane wit and cynicism. She began her career in 1916 when she sold some of her poetry to *Vogue* magazine and was given work as a caption writer. Before long she was writing the satirical book reviews in *The New Yorker* and *Esquire* which first made her famous.

Boris Pasternak (1890–1960) USSR
Poet, novelist and translator. Born in Moscow of artistic parents (his father was a painter and his mother a pianist), he knew Tolstoy and Rilke. During World War I he was sent to work in a factory in the Urals and after the 1917 Revolution ws employed as a librarian in the Ministry of Education. He wrote lyric poetry throughout his adult life; under the new Soviet regime with its socialist realist aesthetic, his works were harshly criticised for being 'non-political'. Author of the novel *Dr Zhivago* (1958).

Lenrie Peters (1932–) Gambia
Poet and novelist. Following a private education in Freetown, Sierra Leone, he

studied medicine in the UK and worked as a surgeon in Northampton Hospital 1966–1969. He continued to practise as a surgeon upon his return to the Gambia, while writing the novel *The Second Round* (1965) and several volumes of poetry, including *Satellites* (1967) and *Katchikali* (1981). He now lives in Banjul, the place of his birth.

Sylvia Plath (1932–1963) USA
Born in Boston, she studied at Smith College and came to England to attend Cambridge University where she met and married the poet Ted Hughes. Poetry collections include *Colossus* (1960), the posthumous *Ariel* (1965) and *Winter Trees* (1971). She committed suicide soon after the publication of her first novel, *The Bell Jar* (1963).

Po Chü–I (772–846) China
After studying at the Han Lin Academy, he retired for four years' customary mourning following the death of his mother and then returned to court. In 814 he was banished but he was later appointed Governor of Hanchow and Soochow provinces. Ill-health caused him to leave these posts and after a period of recuperation he became Governor of Ho-Nan, living in the capital Lo-Yung until his death. He wrote many topographical poems.

Alexander Pope (1688–1744) England
Poet and satirist. A Roman Catholic, he was barred from university by his religion and had little formal education beyond learning Latin and Greek from a local priest as a boy. He later became one of the first poets to support himself by his own writings (including translations of Homer) rather than depending on patronage. He took up residence in Twickenham following a ban on Catholics living in central London and there devoted himself to landscape gardening as well as literature.

Praxilla (c. 450BC–) Greece
Poet who wrote dithyrambs, drinking songs and hymns. The poem included here became proverbial and was quoted by ancient Greek critics as an example of 'nonsense verse' because it mixed the traditional images of the sun and the moon with a reference to cucumbers. Little is known about her life save that she came from Sicyon.

Sheenagh Pugh (1950–) Wales
Lives today near Carmarthen, after growing up in Birmingham of Welsh and Irish parentage. She graduated from Bristol University in Russian and German and later worked in the Welsh Office, Cardiff. Collections include *Crowded by Shadows* (1977), *Earth Studies and Other Voyages* (1982) and *Beware Falling Tortoises* (1987).

Kathleen Raine (1908–) England
Poet, critic and scholar who has written critical works on William Blake as well as three volumes of autobiography and a number of poetry collections. She regards

her early study of natural sciences, together with what she calls 'a sense of the sacred' in the natural world, as important elements in her poetry.

W.S. Rendra (1935–) Indonesia
From Solo in central Java.

Eldred Revett (fl. 1657) England
Landscape poet who published *Poems*, a 165-page volume, in London in 1657. His work has received very little critical attention. He is known to have been a friend of the poet Richard Lovelace and to have mixed in painters' circles.

Cassiano Ricardo (1895–1974) Brazil
One of Brazil's best-known writers, he was a prolific poet and a leading proponent of literary nationalism. He began writing poetry at the age of 10 and published his first collection *Inside of Night* (1915) while a law student. In 1923 he formed a literary group, 'Anta', which helped introduce modernist theories into Latin American writing.

Adrienne Rich (1929–) USA
Poetry collections include *Diving into the Wreck: Poems 1971–72* (1973) and *The Dream of a Common Language: Poems 1974–1977*. She is also well-known for prose works such as *Of Woman Born: Motherhood as Experience and Institution* (1976) and *Compulsory Heterosexuality and Lesbian Existence* (1979), and has translated poetry from Russian and Dutch. She has worked as a creative writing teacher in various colleges and now lives in California.

Rainer Maria Rilke (1875–1926) Austria/Czechoslovakia
Born in Prague, of German descent, he wrote in Italian, French and Russian as well as German. He spent much of his life wandering Europe, finally settling in seclusion in Switzerland where he died prematurely from leukaemia. He distrusted language and deliberately cultivated what he called 'the child's wise incapacity to understand', but eventually found confidence in himself as a 'worthy sounding-board for nature'.

Theodore Roethke (1908–1963) USA
Published 11 volumes of poetry during his lifetime; two more appeared posthumously, as did *Collected Poems* (1966). He grew up in the Detroit area, studied at Harvard and later worked as a lecturer in English at the University of Washington from 1947 unitl his death. He first made his name with *The Waking* (1953) which won a Pulitzer Prize. His late poems are suffused with the atmosphere of the Pacific Northwest.

Wendy Rose (1948–) USA
Poet who also writes under the pen name ChronKahn Shendel. Her works include *Speaking for Ourselves* (1970), *Literature of the American Indian* (1971) and *Hopi Roadrunner Dancing* (1978). She is also a respected artist and edits *American Indian*

Quarterly. She lives and works in California where she earlier trained as an anthropologist.

Alice Sandongei, USA
She is from the Kiowa/Papago tribe and began writing at the age of 14. She lives today in Phoenix, Arizona, and writes, she says, 'about what is familiar, about being Indian'.

Sappho (mid-7th century BC) Greece
Little is known about her life except that she was born on the island of Lesbos, was held in high-esteem as a poet and that young women from leading families gathered around her to study. She then appears to have fled to Sicily, probably following political upheavals, where she later died.

Anna Seward (1747–1809) England
Known as 'The Swan of Lichfield' after the town where she lived for most of her life with her clergyman father. She began writing poetry early and later became a copious letter writer. She bequeathed her works to Sir Walter Scott who edited and published them following her death. Some critics credit her with inventing the epic elegy as a form.

Percy Bysshe Shelley (1792–1822) England
The son of a wealthy landowner, he was originally destined to become an MP like his father but chose to rebel. He was expelled from Oxford for his pamphlet *The Necessity of Atheism* (1811), and went on to write tracts on Ireland, vegetarianism and the free press, as well as the poetry for which he is better known. He eventually left England, travelling in Europe with his second wife, Mary Wollstonecraft, and eventually settling with her in Italy. He drowned when his sailing boat capsized during an Adriatic storm.

Stevie Smith (1902–1971) England
Worked as a secretary in a London publishing company and later as an occasional BBC broadcaster as well as writing poetry, three novels and various short stories and essays. Eight volumes of poetry appeared during her lifetime, including the popular *Not Waving But Drowning* (1957), typical of her verse, with its caustic wit and accompanying comic drawings.

Gary Snyder (1930–) USA
San Francisco poet and writer. His work is much admired by many in the ecology movement, and he has been dubbed a 'theorist of a new pastoral ideology'. He spent some years in Japan studying Buddhism after taking a degree in Japanese and Chinese literature. In the USA he held various jobs, including sailor and forester, prior to a brief period of teaching at the University of California. Verse includes *Riprap* (1959), *The Blue Sky* (1969) and *Turtle Island* (1974).

Edith Södergran (1892–1923) Scandinavia
Born in St Petersburg into a family belonging to the Swedish-speaking minority of Finland, in 1909 her home fell under the rule of the Tsar of Russia. She wrote her early poetry in German, French and Russian, before turning to her mother-tongue to introduce modernist poetry to Scandinavia (for which contemporary critics ridiculed her). She spent most of her short life in poverty and ill-health, dying of malnutrition and tuberculosis at thirty-one.

Wallace Stevens (1879–1955) USA
Trained as a lawyer before joining the legal staff of a Connecticut insurance company, eventually becoming a business executive. His first collection sold less than 100 copies but was praised by some critics; later works like *The Man With the Blue Guitar and Other Poems* (1937) increased his reputation, but it was only in the last years of his life, beginning with *Collected Poems* (1954), that he received the recognition accorded him today.

Alfonsina Storni (1878–1917) Argentina
Born in Switzerland, she was one of the foremost twentieth-century Latin American poets. She lived in Buenos Aires and was one of the few women to take part in the intellectual and literary life of the capital. Her haunted last poetry was collected in *Death-Mask and Clover* in 1938.

Edward Thomas (1878–1917) England
He earned his living by writing volumes of prose, mainly biographical and topological, before turning to poetry with the encouragement of the US poet Robert Frost. Most of his verse appeared posthumously after he was killed in action during World War I. He was born in London but later lived in the Kent countryside.

R.S. Thomas (1913–) Wales
Poet and Anglican priest from Cardiff. He learnt Welsh in order to work in remote rural parishes in the Church of Wales until retiring in 1978; he now lives in Gwynedd. His first poetry collection *Stones of the Field* (1946) was followed by many others, amongst them the popular *Selected Poems 1946–1968* (1973). He has also edited various anthologies, including *The Penguin Book of Religious Verse* (1963).

James Thomson (1700–1748) Scotland (*The Seasons*)
Poet and dramatist. He studied theology at Edinburgh University, where he joined the literary club and published his first poems. He discontinued what was to be a career in the Church after his professor found his sermons 'too imaginative', and worked as a tutor in London instead, becoming a friend of the English poets Pope and Gay. Works include several tragedies, a long allegorical poem, *The Castles of Indolence* (1748) and the poem for which he is best remembered, *The Seasons* (1728–1730).

James Thomson (1834–1882) Scotland (*The City of Dreadful Night*)
Born in Port Glasgow, he was educated in army schools following the death of both of his parents. He worked as an army schoolmaster until alcoholism lost him his post, then as secretary to a goldmining company in North America and as a reporter in Spain for a New York newspaper. He spent the last ten years of his life in England writing *The City of Dreadful Night and Other Poems* (1880) as well as much prose, often under the pseudonym B.V., in the *National Reformer* magazine.

Henry Thoreau (1817–1862) USA
Spent almost all his life in his hometown of Concord, Massachusetts, where he opened his own school, run according to Transcendentalist principles (q.v. Emerson) and advocated civil disobedience against unjust authority (he was jailed for refusing to pay taxes). *Walden, or Life in the Woods* (1854) was the outcome of two years he spent practising self-sufficiency in a hut in woods on the edge of the pond near Concord. He made almost no money from literature and little of his writing was published before his death. Verse includes the posthumous collection *Poems of Nature* (1895).

Charles Tomlinson (1927–) England
Poet, translator and artist. Born in Stoke-on-Trent, the son of a clerk, he studied at Cambridge and London universities and later taught at Bristol University. His poetry first gained recognition in the USA with the publication of *Seeing is Believing* (1958). He collaborated with the Mexican poet Octavio Paz on the sonnet sequence 'Hijos del Aire/Airborn' (1981) and is well known for his translations of both Paz and Antonio Machado.

Tomas Tranströmer (1931–) Sweden
Poet and practising psychologist who worked in prisons for many years. Originally from Stockholm, he travelled widely to give poetry readings and now lives in a small town west of the capital with his family. Collections include *Night Vision* (1970 tr. 1971), *Baltics* (1974, tr. 1975), *The Wild Market Place* (1983, tr. 1985); the US poet Robert Bly has translated some of his work.

Uvavnuk (fl. 1920) Canada
Shaman singer from the Iglulik people of Hudson Bay, Canada. The *Report of the Fifth Thule Expedition* (Denmark 1927–1930) by Gyldendal describes song festivals in which spirits are called up with drums, and how Uvavnuk burst into song about 'all that moved and made her a shaman' after being struck by a meteor. But, continues the report, the unusual thing about Uvavnuk was that 'as soon as she came out of the trance . . . the light left her and she was once more quite an ordinary person with no special powers'.

Virgil (70–19BC) Rome
Highly influential poet who began by writing within the conventions of Greek poetry, and then increasingly made his own mark, with a number of innovations

both stylistically and in terms of content. *Eclogues, Georgics* and the epic poem, *The Aeneid*, are among his best-known works.

Arthur Waley (1889–1966) England
Poet and translator of early Chinese and Japanese writing. Following a Cambridge education, he worked in the Print Room of the British Museum where he taught himself the two languages. His translations, starting with the success of *A hundred and seventy Chinese Poems* (1918) made Chinese and Japanese poetry and novels accessible to English-speakers. He also published many works on oriental art, history and culture, but, despite many invitations, he never visited the region.

Alice Walker (1944–) USA
Grew up in Georgia in a family of sharecroppers, educated at Spelman and Sarah Lawrence Colleges and lives today in San Francisco writing and editing full-time. Best-known for her novel *The Color Purple* (1982) which won a Pulitzer Prize and was made into a film, she also writes essays collected in *In Search of Our Mothers' Gardens: Womanist Prose* (1983) and poetry, including *Once: Poems* (1968), *Revolutionary Petunias and Other Poems* (1973) and *Horses Make a Landscape Look More Beautiful: Poems* (1984).

Margaret Walker (1915–) USA
Born in Alabama, the daughter of a Methodist minister and a music teacher. She studied for a PhD at the University of Iowa and then worked as a newspaper reporter, magazine editor and social worker before her appointment as Professor of English at Jackson State College, Mississippi in 1949, followed by various other academic posts. She became director of the Institute for the Study of the History, Life and Culture of Black Peoples in 1968.

Robert Penn Warren (1905–) USA
Poet, novelist and critic from Kentucky. He studied at the University of California, Yale and Oxford and participated in the Southern Agrarian movement in his youth. He later taught in US universities where his name became associated with the New Criticism, a school which he founded together with Cleanth Brooks. His first volume of poetry *Thirty Six Poems* (1935) was followed by many others including *Promises: Poems 1954–1956* which was awarded a Pulitzer Prize, as was one of his novels, *All the Kings Men* (1946). He was appointed the first US Poet Laureate in 1986.

Laury Wells (1938–) Australia
Born in Walgett, New South Wales, his father was English and his mother Aborigine. He left school aged 14 after his father died and has worked in the bush and on cattle stations for many years. He has been writing poems and short stories since adolescence.

Elizabeth Weston (1582–1612) England/Bohemia
Of English origin, the daugher of alchemist Edward Kelly, she married a Czech
nobleman and settled in what was then Bohemia. She published a collection of
poems in Latin, *Parthenicon*, in 1606 in Prague. Mother of 7 children, she was
described as the 'tenth muse' and regarded as a phenomenal intellectual.

Walt Whitman (1819–1892) USA
Worked as an office boy, a printer, a school teacher and then journalist, before
assuming the role of a full-time poet. *Leaves of Grass* (1855) promotes his vision of
the poet as national prophet and bard. He suffered a paralytic stroke in 1873 but
afterwards continued to write. A controversial figure during his lifetime, he did not
receive public recognition for his literary work until this century.

Anne Wilson (fl. 1778) England
Nothing is known of the author of 'Teisa', an elaborate topographical survey in
verse of the course of the English River Tees. A short biographical passage refers to
her 'humble lot' and laments 'That in a hir'd house all my days are spent'. (see
Eighteenth Century Women Poets ed. Lonsdale 1988)

William Wordsworth (1770–1850) England
Leading Romantic poet whose works include *The Lyrical Ballads* (1798), *Imitations of
Immortality* (1807) and *The Prelude* (1850). He was born in Cumberland and educated at Cambridge before travelling to France, inspired by the 1789 Revolution. He
returned to England, however, disillusioned with the excesses of the Republicans.
Lived much of his life with his wife and cousin, Mary, and his sister, Dorothy, in
the Lake District.

Elinor Wylie (1885–1928) USA
Born in New Jersey into a socially prominent Pennsylvania family. Her first book
was published privately and anonymously in England in 1912. For the next seven
years she worked at both poetry and prose and produced 8 volumes. *Nets to Catch
the Wind* was her first and most acclaimed book of poems. *Angels and Earthly
Creatures, Collected Poems* was published posthumously.

W.B. Yeats (1865–1939) Ireland
Highly influential poet, dramatist and critic who played an important role in the
Celtic revival. He helped found an Irish Literary Society in London in 1891 and
then in Dublin the following year and participated in the creation of the Irish
National Theatre. He served as a senator of the Irish Free State 1922–1928.

Andrew Young (1885–1971) Scotland
Born in Elgin, he was ordained first as a minister of the Free Church of Scotland
and then joined the Anglican clergy. He became Vicar of Stonegate, Sussex in 1941
and Canon of Chichester Cathedral in 1948. He wrote prose as well as poetry for
much of his life, beginning with *Songs of Night* (1910).

Ray A. Young Bear (1950–) USA
Born in Iowa of the Sauk and Fox tribe, better known as the Mesquakies. He attended the University of Northern Iowa, Cedar Falls, as an art student, and has been writing successfully since 1966. The publication of *Winter of Salamanda* (1980) brought him wide critical acclaim.

Yüan Chieh (723–772) China

Acknowledgements

Every effort has been made to contact the copyright holders in all material in this book. The editor regrets if there has been any oversight and suggests the publishers be contacted in any such event. We gratefully acknowledge the following permissions:

Anna Akhmatova, 'Distance collapsed in rubble' and 'Tashkent breaks into blossom' by permission of Bloodaxe Books Ltd from *Selected Poems of Anna Akhmatova* translated by Richard McKane (Bloodaxe Books 1989) copyright © this translation Richard MacKane; 'Everything is plundered' by permission of Harper Collins Publishers Ltd from *Selected Poems of Anna Akhmatova* (Collins Harvill 1974).

Paula Gunn Allen, 'Kopis 'taya' by kind permission of Paula Gunn Allen, copyright © Paula Gunn Allen 1988.

Gillian Allnutt, 'Sunart' by kind permission of Gillian Allnutt, copyright © Gillian Allnutt 1991.

Jorge Carrera Andrade, 'Biography for the use of the birds' from *Anthology of Contemporary Latin American Poetry* (New Directions 1942) translated by Donald Devenish Walsh, by kind permission of New Directions Publishing Corporation, copyright © this translation Donald Walsh 1942.

Anon (Eskimo), 'Delight in nature' from *Eskimo Poems from Canada and Greenland* (Allison and Busby 1973) translated by Tom Lowenstein, by permission Tom Lowenstein, copyright © this translation Tom Lowenstein.

Anon (Eskimo), 'Far inland' from *The Book of Women Poets from Antiquity to Now* (Schocken Books 1981) edited by Aliki Barnstone and Willis Barnstone, copyright © 1980 by Schocken Books Inc. Reprinted by permission of Schocken Books, published by Pantheon Books, a division of Random House Inc.

Anon (Ewe), 'The sky' from *Poems from Africa* (Crowell 1973) edited by S. Allen, copyright © this translation Kafu Hok.

Anon (Medieval Latin), from 'The Cambridge songs' from *The Book of Women Poets from Antiquity to Now* (Schocken Books 1981) edited by Aliki Barnstone and Willis Barnstone, copyright © 1980 by Schocken Books Inc. Reprinted by permission of Schocken Books, published by Pantheon Books, a division of Random House Inc.

Anon (Mudbara), 'The day breaks' from *Primitive Song* (Weidenfeld and Nicolson 1962) C.M. Bowra, copyright © this translation by C.M. Bowra.

Anon (Yoruba), 'Riddles' from *Yoruba Poetry* edited and translated by Ulli Beier (Cambridge University Press 1970), by permission Cambridge University Press, copyright © Ulli Beier.

Anyte, 'Lounge in the shade', from *Sappho and the Greek Lyric Poets* translated by Willis

Index of Poets

Akhmatova, Anna, 90, 91, 175
Al-Mu'ti Hijází, Ahmad 'Abd, 33
Al-Simak, 'Abd Allah ibn, 11
Allen, Paula Gunn, 96
Allnutt, Gillian, 133
Andrade, Jorge Carrera, 35
Anon, Eskimo/Inuit, 50
Anon, Eskimo/Inuit, 92
Anon, Ewe, 168
Anon, King James Bible, 207
Anon, Medieval Latin, 39
Anon, Mudbara, 162
Anon, Yoruba, 161
Anyte, 108
Atwood, Margaret, 199
Awoonor-Williams, George, 49
Barnes, William, 100
Basho, 27
Bellerby, Frances, 88
Bernstein, Marion, 73
Berry, Wendell, 56
Bethell, Mary Ursula, 141
Bishop, Elizabeth, 120, 157
Bly, Robert, 163
Brew, Kwesi, 205
Brontë, Charlotte, 88
Broumas, Olga, 14, 165
Byron, George Gordon, 93
Cardenal, Ernesto, 68
Carter, Elizabeth, 59
Carver, Raymond, 184
Cassian, Nina, 208
Cavafy, C.P., 154
Chaucer, Geoffrey, 10
Clampitt, Amy, 139
Clare, John, 15, 41, 85
Clark, John Pepper, 154
Clarke, Gillian, 172
Coatsworth, Elizabeth, 158
Cotton, Charles, 67

Cowley, Abraham, 25
Cowper, William, 16
Crabbe, George, 201
Crucefix, Martyn, 81
Darwish, Mahmud, 193
Davies, J. Kitchener, 136
Davies, W.H., 28
Davis, Thadious M., 76
Dickinson, Emily, 128, 153, 166, 188
Dobson, Rosemary, 121
Douris, 47
Drayton, Michael, 19, 45
Drummond, William, 102
dsh, 156
Dunmore, Helen, 55, 173
Emerson, Ralph Waldo, 134
Enzensberger, Hans Magnus, 144
Fainlight, Ruth, 171, 192
Fanthorpe, U.A., 181
Feinstein, Elaine, 200
Finch, Anne, 129
Flint, Rose, 129
Goethe, J. W. von, 128
Gould, Janice, 34
Graham, W.S., 51
Greenlaw, Lavinia, 195
Grimké, Angelina Weld, 143
Gurney, Ivor, 106
H.D., 65
Hamburger, Michael, 176
Hardy, Thomas, 202
Heaney, Seamus, 165, 175
Hikmet, Nazim, 3
Holden, Molly, 122, 140
Hölderlin, Friedrich, 21
Hopkins, Gerard Manley, 15, 26, 31
Horovitz, Frances, 185, 186
Hsü Ling, 151
Hughes, Langston, 5
Hughes, John Ceiriog, 50

Issa, 200
Jastrun, Mieczyslaw, 91
Jones, David, 191
Juvenal, 74
Keats, John, 93
Leapor, Mary, 103
Lee, Joyce Isabel, 98
Levertov, Denise, 13, 189
Lochhead, Liz, 123, 178
Logan, Maria, 68
Lowther, Pat, 115
MacCaig, Norman, 151
MacDiarmid, Hugh, 7, 195
Machado, Antonio, 194
Magill, Patrick, 67
Malczewski, Antoni, 189
Marvell, Andrew, 63
McKay, Claude, 41, 86
Mew, Charlotte, 58, 196
Meyette, Terri, 80
Milosz, Czeslaw, 138
Milton, John, 102, 203
Morales, Rosario, 162
Murray, Les A., 152
Murray, Tom, 57
Neruda, Pablo, 127, 159
Nicholson, Norman, 61
Nowlan, Alden, 12, 176
Parker, Dorothy, 32
Pasternak, Boris, 8
Peters, Lenrie, 104
Plath, Sylvia, 78, 118, 147
Po Chü-I, 108, 117
Pope, Alexander, 63
Praxilla, 14
Pugh, Sheenagh, 79, 142
Raine, Kathleen, 3, 95
Rendra, W.S., 190

Revett, Eldred, 154
Ricardo, Cassiano, 32
Rich, Adrienne, 46, 143
Rilke, Rainer Maria, 89
Roethke, Theodore, 111
Rose, Wendy, 20, 40
Sadongei, Alice, 160
Sappho, 18
Seward, Anna, 71
Shelley, Percy Bysshe, 17
Smith, Stevie, 57, 64, 180, 187
Snyder, Gary, 164
Södergran, Edith, 167
Stevens, Wallace, 148
Storni, Alfonsina, 198
Thomas, Edward, 107
Thomas, R.S., 78, 158
Thomson, James (1700–1748), 26, 205
Thomson, James (1834–1882), 197
Thoreau, Henry, 10, 105
Tomlinson, Charles, 99, 138
Tranströmer, Tomas, 159
Uvavnuk, 6
Virgil, 43
Walker, Alice, 142
Walker, Margaret, 13, 36, 75
Warren, Robert Penn, 206
Wells, Laury, 167
Weston, Elizabeth, 48
Whitman, Walt, 6
Wilson, Anne, 23
Wordsworth, William, 23
Wylie, Elinor, 131
Yeats, William Butler, 87
Young, Andrew, 185
Young Bear, Ray A., 183
Yüan Chieh, 99

Index of First Lines

A gardyn saw I ful of blosmy bowes, 10
A man, a field, silence – what is there to
  say?, 78
A sun setting on a wintry horizon, 33
After I came back from Iceland, 79
After the last gapped wire on a post, 152
air hangs like metal, 185
Alone in the woods I felt, 57
Always in observing nature, 128
And when summer comes to an end, 208
Another part, in squadrons and gross bands,
  203
As if somebody ordered it, 90
As imperceptibly as Grief, 166
Ask for what end the heav'nly bodies shine,
  63
At home the sea is in the town, 49
At low tide like this how sheer the water is,
  157
At our feet they lie low, 181
Autumn burns me with, 104
Bananas ripe and green, and ginger root, 41
Because we live in the browning season, 96
Blazing in Gold and quenching in Purple,
  153
Bulkely, Hunt, Willard, Hosmer, Meriam,
  Flint, 134
Clouds of the heavens, 47
Come hither, ye who thirst, 85
Deep within the backlands I walked along
  the road, 32
Distance collapsed in rubble and time was
  shaken, 175
Durst I expostulate with *Providence*, 67
Earth has not anything to show more fair, 23
Ever since the great planes were murdered at
  the end of the gardens, 196
Everything is plundered, betrayed, sold, 91
Far inland, 50
Far spread the moory ground, a level scene, 41

Flat footed plains child, 98
For all frozen things, 173
Glimpsed from the wrong side of a
  motorway, 176
God, I have sought you as a fox seeks
  chickens, 12
Green and differences of green, 122
Harshness gone. And sudden mitigation, 89
Having unbuckled themselves, 20
He heard the corn-buntin' cry 'Guid-night',
  7
He never felt twice the same about the
  flecked river, 148
Health from the lover of the country, me, 25
Here in this valley of discreet academies, 118
here it is bright, by the rusty water,
  nowhere, here, 144
How good it was then to go out into
  quietness, 8
How often I turn round, 185
I am driving; it is dusk; Minnesota, 163
I am not concerned at all with the golden
  age of those pines, 91
I am not suited for service in a country
  town, 108
I am so thankful I have seen, 142
I beheld the earth, and, lo, 207
I believe a leaf of grass is no less than the
  journey-work of the stars, 6
I drove down the Freeway, 164
I go from the woods into the cleared field,
  56
I have had enough, 65
I have just seen a beautiful thing, 143
I have lived in a single landscape. Every
  tone, 138
I'll sing a song of Glasgow town, 73
I love the English country scene, 64
I loved you dearly, Stone Fish Lake, 99
I may be smelly and I may be old, 180

I never may turn the loop of a road, 32

I remember in October, 34

I remember the little disturbances of stone, 133

I've led you by my garrulous banks, babbling, 178

I waded, deepening, into the dark water, 184

I wanted to be a nature poet, 76

I was born in the century of the death of the rose, 35

I will arise and go now, and go to Innisfree, 87

Ibadan, running splash of rust, 154

If I am aware, then the notes come, 129

In plaintive sounds, that tun'd to woe, 59

In September more coyotes were seen, 68

In such a night, when every louder wind, 129

In this country there is neither measure nor balance, 147

In this part of the country, 171

Isn't it delightful, 92

It is a formal and deserted garden, 187

It is a storm-strid night, winds footing swift, 202

It is an isle under Ionian skies, 17

It's not the four-wheeled drive crawler, 55

It started with the polar ice caps, 195

It was a language of water, light and air, 99

Just for the sake of recovering, 51

Just north of town, 115

Leave Krete and come to this holy temple, 18

Let me stop here. Let me, too, look at nature awhile, 154

Lounge in the shade of the luxuriant laurel's, 108

Low-anchored cloud, 10

Luxurious man, to bring his vice in use, 63

make a change, 123

Moonlit evening, silver clear, 167

Most beautiful of things I leave is sunlight, 14

Mountain stream, clear and limpid, wandering down towards, 50

My aspens dear, whose airy cages quelled, 31

My child in the smoke of the fire, 199

My guardian, bear me on thy downy wing, 103

My heart warms under snow, 13

My mother, 160

My roots are deep in southern life; deeper than John Brown, 75

My windows now are giant drops of dew, 28

'Nature' is what we see, 128

Never forget, 200

No lame excuses can gloss over, 78

Nor rural sights alone, but rural sounds, 16

Not an avenue and not a bower, 165

Now nearer, crowns with her enclosure green, 102

O fortunate old man! whose farm remains, 43

Of Albion's glorious Ile the wonders whilst I write, 19

Old fir, young fir, 165

One night of tempest I arose and went, 158

Our skin loosely lies, 40

Out there. The mind of the river, 46

Plac'd on yon fair though beetle brow, 154

Repeat that, repeat, 15

Resting by the water-side, 3

Return me, oh sun, 127

Scene of superfluous grace, and wasted bloom, 71

Scrabble of pencil marked it on the map, 121

Scummed maunderings that nothing loves but reeds, 139

She gave me childhood's flowers, 95

Shout into leaping wind, 13

Some day, when trees have shed their leaves, 86

Speak of the North! A lonely moor, 88

sun (concrete poem by dsh), 156

That spring was late. We watched the sky, 172

The ancient night and the unruly salt, 159

The City is of Night; perchance of Death, 197

The colour of a bayonet this river, 176

The crags crash to the tarn; slow, 61

The day breaks – the first rays of the rising Sun, stretching her arms, 162

The field is trampled over utterly, 192
The fiery palm tree in front of me, 194
The fish faced into the current, 175
The forests of the, 198
The garden of green hillocks, 11
The gentle slopes are green to remind you, 191
The great sea stirs me, 6
The land of Y Llain was on the high marsh, 136
The land wrote itself before any, 142
The Loch of the Wolf's Pass, 151
The night draws in with the setting sun, 167
The pieces of unprofitable land, 140
The poetry of the earth is never dead, 93
The rain has come, and the earth must be very glad, 106
The road that I came by mounts eight thousand feet, 151
The rustling of leaves under the feet and under hedges, 15
The sea is enormous, but calm with evening and sunset, 158
The sky at night is like a big city, 168
The things that give such pleasure to the eye, a clothesline, 14
The track is cleared, 57
The unkind skies have called up angry winds, 48
The very leaves of the acacia-tree are London, 3
The very sea will turn against you, 195
The warriors gone, these fields are void and still, 189
The wet twilight calms the burning forest, 190
The wind leapt, mad-wolf, over the rim of the moor, 88
The year is withering; the wind, 205
There are those to whom place is unimportant, 111
There is a pleasure in the pathless woods, 93
There's a certain Slant of light, 188
There was a time! that time the Muse bewails, 68
They are cutting down the great plane-trees at the end of the garden, 58

They say no one died, 80
They stopped bombing the lake with lime, 81
This darksome burn, horseback brown, 26
This is the grass your feet are planted on, 143
Thrise happie hee, who by some shadie Grove, 102
Thus by himself compell'd to live each day, 201
Tired of all who come with words, words but no language, 159
'Tis raging noon; and, vertical, the sun, 205
To fling my arms wide, 5
To thy loved haunt return, my happy Muse, 26
Today I think, 107
Tonight I think this landscape could, 200
Toward sun, the sun flared suddenly red, 206
Traveller take heed for journeys undertaken in the dark of the year, 36
Up and up, the Incense-burner Peak!, 117
We are entitled to love the end of this autumn and ask, 193
We call the dead – they answer, 161
We have overshot the wood, 186
What is Geography?, 120
What is the name of the tree that blossoms in the subtropical spring, 162
When first religion with a golden chayne, 45
When I am very earnestly digging, 141
When the world turns completely upside down, 131
When zummer's burnen het's a-shed, 100
'White phosphorous, white phosphorous, 189
Who fears in country towns a house's fall, 74
Who is there, 183
Wind is thin, 39
Within the circuit of this plodding life, 105
Year's end, 27
Yes, it is true that the landscape changed a little, 138
Yonder behold a little purling rill, 23
You firmly built alps, 21
You speak of the road in your verses, you picture the joy of it still, 67

Also of interest

THE VIRAGO BOOK OF LOVE POETRY
Edited by Wendy Mulford

For centuries women have written about love with passion, humour, frustration and despair; but never before have their voices come together as in this exhilarating and timeless compendium. Here are love poems in all their true, subversive drama, delicately arranged according to a balance of moods and modes: of argument and lyric, joke and passionate utterance, rejection, rage and ecstasy.

Poets, well-known and obscure, ancient and modern – from Sappho to Akhmatova, Bessie Smith to Selima Hill, Sylvia Plath to Alice Walker – all challenge the traditional perception of woman as muse and object of desire, and magnificently transcend it.

AIN'T I A WOMAN!
Poems by Black and White Women

Collected by Illona Linthwaite

Singing out their triumphs, testifying to the pain and frustration of
past and present struggles, these voices of black and white women
poets echo across the centuries and around the world: from Sappho's
Greece to tenth-century Japan, from nineteenth-century Chile to
Zindziswa Mandela's twentieth-century South Africa. Poets known
and unknown – among them Sherley Anne Williams, Judith
Kazantzis, Grace Nichols, Deborah Levy, Gwendolyn Brooks, Irina
Ratushinskaya – pursue themes of love, injustice, motherhood and
loss, the oppressions of race and sex. Illona Linthwaite began gathering
this collection several years ago, initially for a theatrical performance
which toured Britain. Here, in this unique exchange between women
of many races, affirming their differences and what they have in
common, are more than 150 poems which cajole, bedevil, defy and
in myriad ways, assert the black abolitionist Sojourner Truth's
challenge, 'Ain't I a Woman'.

NAMING THE WAVES
Contemporary Lesbian Poetry

Edited by Christian McEwen

Love and desire, childhood and children, the value of sisterhood, self-identity and racism, day-to-day pleasures and sorrows, the overarching reality of lesbian oppression – and defiance of that oppression: these are the themes of this vibrant collection of contemporary lesbian poetry from both sides of the Atlantic. Here too is a naming and celebrating of difference in the sense of recognising, giving form to what was always there. *Naming the Waves* includes more than 70 poets, both known and unknown: among them are Mary Dorcey, U.A. Fanthorpe, Irena Klepfisz, Audre Lorde, Suniti Namjoshi, Adrienne Rich, Sapphire, Marg Yeo, and many more. In poems that are wonderfully distinct in form and tone – folksongs, prose poems, sestinas – are many moods: from the rhythmical lament of 'Waulking Song' to the quietly joyful 'leaves and potatoes', from the electrifying fear in 'He Touched Me' to the angry confrontation in 'Some Things about the Politics of Size'. And behind the wit and feistiness, the tenderness and anger, lies work in which 'the clear-eyed child and the outraged adult start to merge', their poems all becoming part of the same endeavour, the telling of important truths.

THE SELECTED POEMS OF ANNE SEXTON

Edited and with an Introduction by Diane Wood Middlebrook and Diana Hume George

Anne Sexton could be called the first poet of contemporary women. She spoke of her life as no woman before her had dared to speak.

Her language was simple, domestic; her imagery arresting; her subject matter urgent, shocking and exciting. She wrote about mental breakdown, sex, addiction, abortion – the other side of ordinary life. Stepping to the podium in the long dresses she wore for public readings, she seemed anything but ordinary. Kicking off her shoes, lighting a cigarette, she would read, in her marvellous, throaty voice, harrowing accounts of insanity and loss. Top fees for her readings were hers for the asking; her friends included Maxine Kumin, Robert Lowell and Sylvia Plath. But fame could not cure her 'madness' and in October 1974, aged 45, she committed suicide.

This selection celebrates one of America's most widely-read poets, at the height of her remarkable powers.

Virago also publish *Anne Sexton: A Biography* by Diane Wood Middlebrook.